Praise for
The Quick and Easy Performance Appraisal Phrase Book

"*The Quick and Easy Performance Appraisal Phrase Book* has... everything you need to deliver powerful evaluations."

–Onnik Tchulluian, manufacturing manager at St. Jude Medical

"I use this book [regularly] for managing my staff. You will praise the day you found this amazing tool."

–Céline Lacote, director of Quality Assurance at Coromega

"The definitive tool for helping managers who must retain or remonstrate employees."

–David Amsellem, CEO at Manager4less.com

"This book will make your appraisal process easy, fast, and productive."

–Danny J. Fuleihan, chief operating officer at Softensity, Inc.

"*The Quick and Easy Performance Appraisal Phrase Book* covers all aspects of appraisals, including how to wake up your subordinates with harsh rhetoric, if necessary."

–Basil Abbas, CEO at Tecsol Software

The Quick and Easy

Performance Appraisal Phrase Book

3,000+ Powerful Phrases for Successful
Reviews, Appraisals, and Evaluations

By Patrick Alain

CAREER
PRESS
Pompton Plains, NJ

THE QUICK AND EASY PERFORMANCE APPRAISAL PHRASE BOOK
TYPESET BY DIANA GHAZZAWI
Cover design by Jeff Piasky
Printed in the U.S.A.

To order this title, please call toll-free 1-800-CAREER-1 (NJ and Canada: 201-848-0310) to order using VISA or MasterCard, or for further information on books from Career Press.

CAREER
PRESS

The Career Press, Inc.
220 West Parkway, Unit 12
Pompton Plains, NJ 07444
www.careerpress.com

Library of Congress Cataloging-in-Publication Data
Alain, Patrick.
    The quick and easy performance appraisal phrase book: 3000+ powerful phrases for successful reviews, appraisals, and evaluations / by Patrick Alain.
        pages cm
    Includes index.
    ISBN 978-1-60163-267-8 (pbk.) -- ISBN 978-1-60163-526-6 (ebook)
    1. Employees--Rating of. 2. Employees--Rating of--Terminology. I. Title.

HF5549.5.R3A39 2013
658.3'125014--dc23

2013000074

To my wife, Zaina.

Acknowledgments

I wish to first thank my in-laws, Sam and Lina Abi-Samra, for their unflagging belief that I am saving the world one phrase at a time. I cannot thank them enough for showing me what it means to be present.

I would like to thank my wife, Zaina, for standing beside me throughout the writing of this book. She has been my inspiration and motivation for continuing to broaden my knowledge and move my writing career forward. She is my rock.

I also thank my beautiful daughter, Michèle, for her understanding that when I'm writing, I'm unable to give her my undivided attention. I hope that she will one day read my books and finally understand why I spent so much time secluded in front of the computer.

I would also like to acknowledge my friend, Tom Carroll, without whom this book series would never have seen the light of day. It was Tom who served as a sounding board for many of the phrases that are found in the three books that now make up the series.

Last, but truly not least, I owe the very existence of my books to my literary agent, Jessica Faust. Jessica, this never would have happened without you. Thanks, too, to my developmental editor, Kirsten Dalley, for finding this book in me, one that I didn't believe existed, and for all your edits, input, and vision, and for skillfully shepherding the manuscript into fruition. And I would be remiss if I did not thank my publicist, Tess Woods, for her guidance in getting the word out about what I hope will be a very helpful tome.

Contents

Preface

I wrote this book as a powerful framework for managers to use when it comes time for the dreaded performance review. The fact that you're reading this book probably means that you would like to communicate more effectively as a manager during these critical junctures. Or perhaps you just want to perfect your communication skills so you'll be eligible for a management position down the line. Either way, this book is for you!

Most managers view performance appraisals with the same amount of excitement and anticipation as their inferiors do—that is to say, with very little of either. In order to provide an employee with an effective and useful review, a manager must develop a strong foundation of communication skills. This is critical for achieving a successful outcome, whether the review is positive or negative. Sure, it can be daunting to have to critique an employee on his or her hygiene, but this book is all about overcoming exactly those kinds of challenges. After all, the whole purpose of the review is to provide employees with the feedback necessary for them to carve a brighter pathway to a more successful future.

Successful performance appraisals start here, with the powerful phrases you need to get your message across. Ready? Let's begin!

How to Use This Book

This book was designed with flexibility in mind. You can read it all the way through to get a general overview, or you can work on one particular situation or issue that may be presenting itself in an upcoming performance review that promises to be challenging. For example, you may feel very comfortable reviewing an employee's general quality of work, but you may not feel as relaxed when doling out criticism about tardiness or a lack of personal grooming. Use the in-depth index at the back of the book to help you find the topic that is most applicable to each situation.

Read all the sample phrases and make a point to familiarize yourself with the ones that feel the most natural or comfortable. Then, practice them until they flow naturally from your mouth—or your pen (if you are writing the review). When the time comes you'll have no trouble summoning them and using them with confidence and aplomb. And because everyone couches things in a slightly different way, there's a bit of space in the margins where you can amend the existing phrases or add your own favorites. When you are giving the review in person, though, the right words won't necessarily be enough: Remember that tone, body language, and timing (context) are all important in conveying meaning and in how your statements will be taken by others. Thus, a humorous phrase that would be effective and appropriate in one setting could be construed as hostile and inappropriate in another, depending on how, when, and to whom it is said. Always use good judgment and let context be your guide. This is particularly important when you are considering using humor or sarcasm to get a point across. Humor can sometimes come across as flip or dismissive, and sarcasm is definitely

Conciliatory

one of the quickest ways to make someone feel inept and insignificant. Not everyone will appreciate your style of delivery, so nuance is always required. As well, written reviews are usually more formal in tone and format than verbal reviews done face-to-face. So again, adjust your wording and tone accordingly.

The continuum accompanying each review issue will help you anchor each "order of magnitude" in your mind, which will then serve as a valuable mnemonic device down the road. For example, in the sample to the left, the continuum indicator goes from **Conciliatory** to **Argumentative**. All of the phrases in this book are presented on a similar scale. In this example, if you wanted to build bridges and/or smooth things over, you would learn and use the phrases toward the top. If you wanted to eliminate the niceties and cut to the chase–and maybe even wield your words as you would a weapon– you would use the phrases toward the bottom.

Finally, I thought it important to note that I am presenting the English language as most people understand and use it today; thus, the reader will find colloquialisms and some slang. Obviously, the use of the idiom will be much different in, say, Canada or Australia, as it will be even in different parts of the States. Ultimately, all languages are living things and in a state of constant flux. Therefore, the material in this book will perforce need updating from time to time, as the way we express ourselves inevitably evolves. Please visit my Website, *www.patrickalain.com,* for the most up-to-date information to add to your linguistic arsenal. I also welcome your comments on, and criticisms of, this work to help me in that process.

Argumentative

Part 1
The Performance Appraisal Meeting

This part of the book is intended to give you talking points as a framework for an actual performance appraisal meeting. This is when you look your employee in the whites of his eyes and tell him how well or how poorly he's been doing over the past year. Because this conversation is obviously fraught with all kinds of perils and pitfalls, I've provided you with some ready-made phrases to help jump-start the process.

One option is to dive right in and tell him how you feel he's been doing. Another and sometimes better option is to invite the employee to open up first: ask him how *he* feels he's been doing. You will be surprised at how frank people can be when you invite them to be open and honest with you. At the very least, you will be encouraging self-awareness on the part of your employee—something that will be sure to benefit him now or down the line.

It should go without saying that you yourself should be 100-percent honest throughout this meeting. But remember, *honest* doesn't always mean "brutally honest." As always, let context be your guide and use your best judgment.

How to Encourage Discussion

Informal

- I'm definitely not the only one with something to say here. What do *you* think?

- This isn't about me. I'm more interested in what you have to contribute.

- Okay, are you ready for our little coffee klatch? [*joking*]

- I know I have a habit of running on, so please feel free to interject whenever you like.

- This is a democracy, not a dictatorship. Your opinion matters, too!

- I want you to think of this as a friendly chat between friends, okay?

- Please feel free to speak your mind; I really mean that!

- I prefer to think of this review as something we are creating together.

- I am all ears–tell me everything that's on your mind.

- This isn't just about me. I'm excited to hear *your* input and feedback.

- I'm really interested to hear where you're coming from in all of this.

- Your thoughts are more important to me than anything, so feel free to speak up.

- There are no wrong answers here; please feel free to speak honestly and openly.

- Everything we discuss here stays here, okay?

- I think it's more important for me to listen than speak; please go ahead and start.

- This is the best place for this kind of discourse. Let's start now.

- I believe it is more than appropriate for you to have a say in this.

- Everyone here has a chance to speak their mind, and this includes you.

- You should feel quite comfortable speaking up in meetings like this.

- Whenever you feel like speaking up, you should.

- Our time will be well-spent if you take the lead and speak up.

- Maybe there are restrictions on speaking your mind at other companies, but not here.

- I'd like to encourage you to share your thoughts and ideas at any time.

- As an employee here, your input is very important to us.

- I would very much like to hear your professional opinion on these issues.

- I believe the best results will come from honest, to-the-point discourse.

Businesslike

How to Encourage Employees to Appraise Themselves

Informal

- I know what I think, but I am more interested in how you perceive your performance.

- If you had to guess, what do you think I would say your strengths and weaknesses are?

- If you could tell me three things about your work style, what would they be?

- So how do you think you've been doing lately?

- My opinion is secondary at best; it's what *you* think of you that counts!

- I know it's tough, but tell me how you think *you're* doing.

- You don't need a higher-up to tell you how you're doing, right?

- I think you know better than anyone else how you've been doing here.

- The best way for us to assess your performance is for you to do a self-check.

- The best way to impress higher-ups is to assess your own work.

- I believe we can be our own toughest critic. What do you think?

- Self-awareness is an important key to success, so tell me how you think you've been doing.

Businesslike

- I believe we all function best when we answer firstly and primarily to ourselves.

- We all need to take an unflinching and honest look at our own work.

- It's important to be able to assess one's self as objectively as possible.

How to Take Control

Casual

- I think it's best to take the bull by the horns—what do you think?

- Let me take the first shot here and then you can get your licks in, I promise. [*joking*]

- No time like the present—let's get started!

- Now you just sit back and let me do all the talking, okay? [*joking*]

- I need to know that you're comfortable being on the receiving end of my critiques today.

- I don't want to appear forceful, but I'd like to say a few things before we get into a discussion.

- When you are ready, I'd like to go through the following items on my agenda.

- I'm not really looking for your input; today it's all about how I feel about your work.

- The important thing here is that you listen carefully to this honest appraisal.

- The best way to accomplish this review is for me to talk and you to listen.

- I know you want to have your voice heard, but I am more comfortable running this review.

- I'd like to keep this meeting short and on-point, so here's what we'll be discussing.

- I'm sure you've got a lot to say, but first you'll need to internalize my feedback.

- The performance review is really about my view of your performance here, correct?

- This meeting will be a success if you simply listen and absorb what I have to say.

- The only thing that matters is how I think you're doing.

- The more you try to direct this meeting, the lower your review score will be.

- Just follow my lead here and we'll have no problems.

- I am not the one being reviewed here.

- Here is how this meeting is going to go.

- Just so we're clear, I'll be directing this meeting.

- I'd like to begin by going over the list of things I want to cover.

Formal

How to Avoid False Starts

Friendly

- Let's make this as quick and painless as possible, okay?

- Let's keep this meeting on track and moving right along, alright?

- I'd really like this to go as smoothly as possible, okay?

- I'd really like to get things off to a smooth start; are you with me?

- Before we begin, do you have any concerns or questions that you'd like to get out on the table?

- So as to prevent any false starts, let's lay out an agenda for what we want to cover.

- I need to know that I will have your buy-in on my feedback. Can we agree on that?

- If we get things off to a rocky start it will only hurt you, you know.

- Once we start, I really want things to go smoothly and without a hiccup.

- With your cooperation, I know we can make this as painless as possible.

- So you don't get the wrong idea, here is a list of exactly what we will be discussing today.

- If at any point you have questions or concerns, please feel free to stop me.

- I want to make sure you're prepared for this meeting before we start.

Businesslike

How to Respond to New Ideas

Praising

- Your ideas are completely inspired. I can't wait to get the next proposal from your team.

- You can't possibly be as inspired as this all the time, but amazingly, it seems that you are.

- Anyone as talented as you are at generating great ideas should have his/her compensation doubled.

- I can't recall the last time I was this excited over a new idea at this company.

- Sometimes I feel as though I can't even get an idea formulated before you present it to me, fully realized.

- Your ability to innovate with spirit and intelligence has really vaulted the company to success.

- Your latest ideas are taking it to a whole new level. I'm making a note of that in your permanent record.

- It's a great feeling to have someone on board with this much initiative and creativity. Keep it up!

- The evidence is in: You are an intelligent employee with a lot of great ideas.

- You've certainly given the department a lot of great notions in the past.

- Idea generation is a real talent, but what really matters is how new ideas work in the real world.

- Turning ideas into actual strategies is what we are looking for. Are you equal to the task?

- Not everyone is adept at innovating; don't let it stop you from continuing to try, though.

- Generating ideas is not just about innate talent. I'd like to see you working harder at this.

- We are all about innovation here, and I'm concerned that I'm not seeing more coming from you.

- Many employees are involved in innovating around here, but you need to step it up.

- If I had to evaluate everyone's ability to generate new ideas, I'd never get anything done.

- I appreciate your enthusiasm, but I'm not sure your ideas are going in the right direction.

- You certainly have a lot of ideas, but I'm not sure if any of them really have any "legs."

- I thought I hired an Idea Guy, but all I got was a Recycle Guy.

- I'm dissapointed that you seem to have neither the talent nor the motivation to innovate.

- I was hoping that you would be able to take the lead here in innovation, but it's not working out.

- If you fail to plan to innovate, you may as well plan to fail here.

- An idea is a terrible thing to waste, but in this case, there are no ideas.

- Is there anything I can do to help prime the idea pump? Because things really need to change.

- You're paid for what you bring to the table here, but I'm not seeing much, if anything.

- Unfortunately I don't see you taking any initiative to contribute anything new around here. I don't think things are working out.

Critical

How to Create a Relaxed Atmosphere

Casual

- First off, I just want to say how much I enjoy working with you. I hope you feel the same!

- I've really been looking forward to our little chat.

- Most of the time meetings like this are painful, but you always make it a pleasure.

- I can't remember when I've had as enjoyable an experience meeting with an employee.

- You make this process easy, so please don't worry a bit!

- It's such a pleasure chatting with you, I wish we could extend our meeting indefinitely.

- Please feel at ease with me and know that you're among friends.

- The feeling here is so positive, I want to bottle it and take it with me to my next meeting.

- This is good Just two professionals hanging out, professionally.

- I wish every meeting could be this easy and carefree.

- I've always enjoyed our meetings, and this time is no exception.

- It's a blessing that we are two like-minded individuals working toward the same goals.

- With some employees this is a tense situation, but it's never that way with you.

- Please sit down and relax a bit before we begin with the more serious stuff.

- Even though I don't know you very well, I feel that we have a good rapport.

- I'm glad we had the opportunity to meet today. I hope you feel comfortable talking to me.

- Okay, let's take care of business first; then we can chat afterward.

- Please make yourself comfortable. How is everything going otherwise?

- I am very pleased with your work, so you can relax and know this meeting will go smoothly.

- It's always a pleasure meeting with you, even when it's review time.

- Although this meeting will be all business, know that I am here to help and encourage you.

- You seem tense, but there is really no need to be. This will all go very well, I'm sure.

- If we are both relaxed we will be able to accomplish so much more during this meeting.

- Please make yourself comfortable. This will not take long, I assure you.

- I know it's difficult, but I'd like you to feel as relaxed as possible during this meeting.

- It is important that we both feel at ease and comfortable discussing the nitty-gritty.

- Whatever is discussed here, stays here, so please feel free to discuss whatever is most pressing.

- I certainly hope you feel comfortable speaking with me about any business issue that may arise.

Formal

How to Put a Nervous Employee at Ease

Informal

- Wow. You're as nervous as a long-tailed cat in a room full of rocking chairs. [*joking*]

- Why so nervous? No one is going to roast you or eat you alive. [*joking*]

- Let's make this as quick and painless as possible—for both of us. [*joking*]

- Let's get this over with so we can go out and grab some lunch afterward!

- This will be a friendly performance review—not the other kind. [*joking*]

- Listen, I know you're a bit nervous. Would you like some water or coffee?

- Consider us friends getting together and catching up after being apart for a while.

- Remember that I am on your side, okay?

- I'm actually a bit nervous, too, if that helps at all.

- Please make yourself comfortable. I want you to feel at ease, okay?

- I want you to know that you are among friends here, okay?

- My main goal in all of this is to see you succeed, as I know you will.

- Let me assure you that you have nothing to worry about.

- You have nothing to fear, from me or anyone else around here.

- While it's natural to be nervous, in your case you really don't need to be.

Formal

- Please don't worry—you're in excellent standing here.
- I know this is not the most pleasant part of the job, but you'll do just fine.
- I'd like to preface this by saying that I am very pleased with your performance
- So as to put your mind at rest, please know that I have only good things to say to and about you.

How to Keep Things Brief

Casual

- I know we're both busy, so let's just cut to the chase.
- Unless you object, we can probably get this meeting over with pretty quickly.
- Let's keep this short and to the point, okay?
- This shouldn't take long at all.
- There are just a couple of things I want to go over with you.
- This shouldn't take more than a few minutes at most.
- Discussing this stuff any longer may violate the law of diminishing returns.
- It would be great to draw this out, but I've got a ton on my plate today.
- We need to keep this meeting on track and on schedule, okay?
- Since there's not a lot of time, let's get to the nitty-gritty right away.

Formal

- I would like to keep this meeting short and sweet. I'm sure you won't object.

- I think we'll be able to accomplish everything pretty quickly today, don't you?

- To expedite things, let's stay on track with each of the items on the agenda.

- We can talk about other, more tangential subjects some other time.

- There is no reason for us to drag this out any longer than we have to.

- I'd like to really stay on task and on schedule today.

- It's important that we use our time here today economically and efficiently.

How to Engage an Employee With Small Talk

Friendly

- How have you been recently? I feel like we never get a chance to chat.

- Let's put our feet up and shoot the breeze a bit before we begin.

- I'm just exhausted today—how about you?

- So, how's the family doing? Any plans for the weekend?

- Did you catch the game/see the new movie last night?

- I like to get to know my employees as real people. What do you do for fun?

- I was thinking we should have a party this year. Any ideas where we should hold it?

- How is everything otherwise? Everything going well at home?

- How was your commute this morning?

- I want to get to know you a bit better. How do you like to spend your free time?

- I know this is a business meeting, but I also want you to know that I care about you as a person.

- I feel like I need to catch up with you personally. What else has been going on?

- I think it's in the "small" talk that we learn the most about one another; wouldn't you agree?

- I don't believe that there is any such thing as small talk, even at work.

- Your performance here is important, but I'm more concerned about you as a person.

- Now that's we've covered the nitty-gritty, how's everything else going?

- I know I can be a bit chatty, but I do enjoy the more personal aspects of my job.

- What else of note is going on in the department? Any changes or improvements?

Businesslike

How to Break Through Defensiveness

Casual

- Look, I've sat where you're sitting and I know it will be okay.

- I am on your side in all of this. I just want to see you fulfill your potential.

- I know this feels terrible. Believe me, I've been there!

- None of us is perfect; it's how we respond to criticism that really matters.

- I would not be telling you this stuff if I did not value you as an employee.

- Please don't get your back up; this kind of thing happens to the best of us.

- Given a little time, you'll feel better about things, I'm sure.

- I'll allow you to feel a bit defensive initially, but I am more interested in how you will address the issue.

- We all have egos to contend with, but I suggest putting yours aside for the moment.

- I know this is a sensitive topic, but we are talking about it because you're a valued employee.

- Please think of this criticism as an opportunity for you to make things better.

- If you could be objective for a few moments, you'd see the truth in what I am saying.

- This is not just my opinion, though; others here have mentioned this, as well.

- If you reach down deep inside, I know you will find the emotional resilience to handle this.

- I know this was hard to hear, but I also know you are wise enough to make the most of it.

Businesslike

How to Address Immediate Confrontation With an Employee

Empathetic

- You are absolutely within your rights to be upset. I know—I've been there, too.

- I can certainly see your point, and I feel confident we can work this out together.

- I feel terrible being the messenger, but please don't kill me! [*joking*]

- I can see that you're upset. Did you want to take a break to cool off for a bit?

- I hate being the bearer of bad news. What can I do to help soften the blow?

- Let's reconvene when we are both feeling a bit calmer and more centered.

- I know you are angry, but please know that this is hard for me, too.

- I'd like to keep this whole process as professional and dispassionate as possible.

- You and I both know you're too wrapped up in this to think rationally right now.

- Why don't we revisit the matter tomorrow? Maybe things will look different then.

- I know you are upset, but it's important that you put your emotions aside for the time being.

- Would it be possible for you to think about this objectively just for a moment?

- It won't help either of us if you cannot get your emotions under control.

Rejecting

- You're angry, I can see that. But you still need to listen to what I have to say.

- When it comes to performance reviews, the feelings of my employees are irrelevant.

- I must tell you truth, regardless of the way you feel.

- Your comfort is not the goal here; giving you an honest appraisal is.

How to Involve Others in the Appraisal

Subtle

- I'm wondering if it might be helpful to hear some other viewpoints.

- Sometimes I think this would be more helpful coming from others.

- I would feel better about this process if others were involved, too. How about you?

- I wonder what so-and-so would have to say about this—should we ask him?

- Let's take a moment to discuss who else might want to be involved in your review.

- I'm sure there are other employees who could weigh in. Let's make a list.

- I think reviews are much more effective when there are other opinions present.

- Is there anyone else you can think of who might want to weigh in on this?

- Whose opinion do you value, who you would like to see at this meeting?

Directive

- I think we need a more complete picture of your performance. Wouldn't you agree?

- I'd like to encourage you to seek out the opinions of others regarding your performance.

- Is there anyone else here who might be able to shed light on this?

- Rather than risking groupthink, let's involve some dissenting opinions. What do you think?

- Is there anyone here who can speak to your specific strengths/weaknesses?

How to Narrow the Focus of the Appraisal

Subtle

- Sometimes you can miss the forest for the trees, but the opposite also holds true.

- If you're handling all the details well, the big picture will take care of itself.

- No one exists in a broad brushstroke world. Everyone has to concentrate on the details.

- If you sweat the small stuff, you'll find the big stuff to be quite manageable.

- A great performance here is made up of small but significant victories, each and every day.

- I often get a more accurate picture of an employee's performance upon closer inspection.

- I wonder if it would be more effective to just focus on one or two specific tasks.

- I am actually most interested in understanding the core or essence of this issue.

- Have you ever heard that saying, God is in the details? That holds true here, too.

- Now that we've looked at the big picture, let's focus on this one specific area.

- Let's take a close look at your day-to-day activities to see how things are going.

- Focusing on just one or two responsibilities will help us see everything more clearly.

- I think we need to zoom in a bit on the fundamentals of what you do.

- Rather than get lost in extraneous details, I'd rather confine our discussion to one topic.

- I'd like to spend most of our time here today looking at your highest-priority task.

Directive

Part 2
Job Skills

If you are appraising a recent hire or someone who's having trouble catching on to the task at hand, this is likely where you will spend the bulk of your energy and time. Most employees will be strong in certain skills and not so strong in others, and it is your job to figure out which one is which. Of course, the value of each of these skills will be contingent on the industry you're in. For example, although creativity may not necessarily be a valued commodity in IT, it is always needed when it comes to problem-solving and dealing with people. Context is key.

Think about the competencies or characteristics that are required for not only surviving, but thriving on the job. With that in mind, pick and choose the skills listed in this section that are most applicable. Of course, if you don't see a particular competency or skill listed here, feel free to add it in the margins. Remember, this is not a one-size-fits-all solution, but a guide that is designed to help jump-start your own creative process.

Appraise an Employee's General Skills

Glowing

- I don't think anyone else here can touch you in terms of the depth and breadth of your skills.

- You have more to offer in terms of general skills than anyone else I have ever managed.

- With your many and diverse skills, I can only say the most glowing things about you.

- With the skills you have, the world is your oyster.

- If I had skills like yours, I would be giving reviews to presidents, CEOs, and senior partners.

- Your skills and your use of them are unimpeachable.

- With your vast array of skills across many areas, you are an asset to this department.

- The only other person I know who has the skills you have is leading this company.

- Your basic skills are excellent and above reproach.

- I can't really think of anything negative to say about your general skills.

- Just keep doing what you're doing.

- Your job skills are, in general, quite good, although a few areas may need some brushing up.

- I have some concerns about your job skills that I need to share with you.

- Here are some ideas for how you could improve your skills and stay more current.

- I'm calling this a "general skills review" because your skills are, in general, pretty marginal.

Critical

- I am concerned that someone with more skills will come along and replace you. How can we avoid that?

- I feel that you've been coasting along at this general skill level. You've got to keep learning to survive.

- I'm honestly not sure how you made it this far with those glaring omissions in your skill set.

- Unless you go for further training, I think we are going to have to reevaluate your position here.

- I am shocked and appalled that you've done nothing to improve your skills since you came aboard.

- Since your skills are obsolete and you show no interest in improvement, we'll have to replace you with someone else.

Appraise an Employee's Analytic Skills

Glowing

- I have never met anyone with such an analytic, logical mind.

- Your skills of analysis and logic have been a great boon to this department and the company.

- Your analytic skills are only matched by the excellent training and experience you've had using them.

- Your accuracy and incisiveness are legendary and to be commended.

- You truly are gifted in the area of analytic reasoning.

- Your reasoning and analytic abilities are what help keep us successful.

- We really could use more left-brain people like you around here!

- Your analytic prowess is simply amazing. Keep up the good work!

- You certainly would have given Einstein a run for his money!

- I'm glad to see that you continually strive to stay sharp with your analytic skills.

- Whatever you lack in innate skills, you've more than made up for with hard work and education.

- Although you're not the most analytic employee I've had, you more than compensate with your emotional intelligence/drive/work ethic.

- It's important that you continue to polish your analytic skills, especially since they are not as sharp as they once were.

- I have concerns about how you've been crunching the numbers lately. Can we talk about that?

- It's important that you be dead accurate in this aspect of your job. How can we improve that?

- I feel as though you've been getting a bit sloppy in your analysis lately, and that concerns me.

- It's imperative that your analytic skills and accuracy improve before your next review.

- It's critical that you address these lapses in your analytic performance here before it's too late.

- I have no use for someone who continually makes such egregious errors and shows no sign of improving.

Critical

Appraise an Employee's Computer Skills

Glowing

- If Steve Jobs and Bill Gates had ever had a child, it would have been you. [*joking*]

- Were you perhaps born with a MacBook Pro in your hands? [*joking*]

- I have nothing but good things to say about your proficiency in the area of IT.

- Someone with your level of skills ought to be starting her own company.

- The fact that you are so tech-savvy is a big part of what makes us so successful.

- There is absolutely nothing you can't do with a computer, is there?

- I have no complaints about your computer skills and knowledge of IT.

- Your computer knowledge is more than adequate for the type of work you're doing.

- You're doing fine right now, but you'll need to keep improving to stay competitive.

- You seem comfortable with a computer, but there are some gaps in your knowledge base.

- You certainly don't know everything about computers, but I like that you've taken the initiative to learn more.

- Computer skills should be a given in this day and age; after all, this is a digital world.

- I am concerned that your lack of technical skills are holding you—and us—back.

Critical

- Being technologically literate is a necessity here; what can we do to improve that area of your job?

- How did you ever make it through school with such a dearth of computer skills?

- Since you obviously have neither the natural inclination nor the drive to learn this stuff, we'll need to rethink your employment here.

Appraise an Employee's Technical Skills

Glowing

- Your technical skills and knowledge are so thorough and complete, I wish you would teach the others.

- You are such a tech wizard, I think I am starting to fear for my job! [*joking*]

- It almost seems as though you were born to excel at the technical aspect of this job.

- You have a ready and comprehensive grasp of all the technical issues involved.

- Your technical skills and knowledge are above reproach. Well done!

- With your technical knowledge and skills, I knew you'd be the perfect person for this job.

- It's important that you feel comfortable with the technical aspect of your job. Do you?

- I don't have any specific complaints about your technical skills, but I would like to see you stay more current.

- You have a basic understand of these technical skills, but I don't see true mastery yet.

- Your grasp of the technical part of this job is pretty good, but I see some room for improvement.

- Technical proficiency is a must in this position—are you up for getting the skills you need to succeed?

- You either know the technology or you don't. Unfortunately, I don't think you do.

- I'm going to give you an opportunity to address your lack of tech skills before your next review.

- I'm really aghast at how much you need to learn to be technically proficient.

- Technology may not be the "be all, end all," but you still need to be literate.

- When I said that this job required an understanding of technology, I meant it.

- What part of "technological proficiency" did you not understand?

- No one can expect to do this job without having at least a moderate understanding of the tech involved.

- As they say, "Without the tech, you're just a wreck."

- With your technical "skills" I can't continue to allow you to bring the department down.

Critical

Appraise an Employee's Knowledge of Job Responsibilities

Glowing

- There is not a single aspect or nuance of your job that you don't get, is there?

- It seems as though you've managed to memorize the entire employee handbook. Amazing!

- Even I don't know my responsibilities and duties as well as you do! [*joking*]

- You have an almost encyclopedic knowledge of your duties; do you have an eidetic memory?

- You seem completely conversant in and comfortable with all of your responsibilities.

- You obviously have a complete and thorough knowledge of what it is you do.

- There is no one here who is more familiar with his or her job requirements.

- I wish the other employees had this kind of thorough knowledge of their responsibilities.

- In general I am pleased with your grasp of your job requirements.

- You've obviously put in a lot of time to learn everything, but I think there is more you need to know.

- You certainly work hard, but you don't always seem entirely clear on your responsibilities and duties.

- I assumed you understood your job requirements here, but maybe I was wrong.

- What you lack in knowledge you (somewhat) make up for in hard work and dedication.

- Can we target your activities here to get them more in line with your job requirements?

- You seem pretty unclear on your job description. How can we fix that before your next review?

- I'm not asking for the minutiae of your job requirements; just a general understanding would suffice.

- There's no sense in working hard if you're not even sure what you should be doing, right?

- I don't understand why you are so confused about your duties and responsibilities.

- I can't continue paying someone who clearly has no idea what's expected of her.

- So, what is your excuse for your lack of knowledge? Don't forget that ignorance is no excuse.

- Without a thorough knowledge of your job duties, how can you possibly expect to keep your job?

- Watching you flounder makes it quite obvious that you haven't the slightest idea of what you're supposed to be doing.

Critical

Appraise an Employee's Organizational Skills

Glowing

- It is so impressive how you have a place for everything and everything in its place.

- I admire how you have created a sanctuary of order in the midst of chaos.

- You are one of the most organized employees I've ever had. I wish everyone were like you!

- I've never once seen you drop the ball when it comes to being organized. How do you do it?

- The way you execute your duties here is methodical, precise, and, above all, highly organized.

- So much of this job depends on the ability to stay organized, and you obviously have no problem with that.

- You are our go-to person when it comes to imposing order on all the confusion.

- I never have to worry that you will be sloppy or forgetful when I delegate tasks to you.

- I know I can always count on you to keep things organized, on track, and on schedule.

- Every team needs at least one player who focuses on orderliness and organization. That is you.

- You're not the most organized employee, but you still manage to keep track of everything.

- I know staying organized doesn't come naturally to you, but I can see that you're trying.

- Sometimes your work style seems a bit chaotic and sloppy, but you always seem to make it work somehow.

Critical

- I can tell that you are struggling with staying organized. How can I help you improve?

- I am wondering if you could bump up your organizational skills just a bit.

- Chaos is starting to encroach on your tasks and workspace. You really need to be more organized.

- I'm concerned that your lack of organization is negatively affecting your performance here.

- Organizing really isn't your thing, is it?

- You need to focus on getting organized if you are going to survive in this department.

- Someone as sloppy and disorganized as you, will never go far here or anywhere else.

Appraise an Employee's Discernment

Glowing

- Your good judgment and discretion have been invaluable to the success of this company.

- I so appreciate the sagacity and good judgment you bring to bear in each and every situation.

- I always appreciate your discernment and discretion in everything you do.

- Thanks to your fine-tuned discernment, you always make the right decision each and every time.

- I wish everyone else were as shrewd and discriminating as you are.

- Your opinion carries the most weight here because of your discernment and acumen.

- I would back you in any decision you make because you always seem to know exactly what to do.

- I rarely see you falter when it comes time to bring your best judgment to bear on a situation or crisis.

- While you have good judgment, sometimes you allow your emotions to get in the way.

- There's a great opportunity to advance if you can start making better decisions.

- You are only as discerning as your last good decision. Just remember that.

- I know you try hard to make good decisions, but sometimes you just don't seem to get it.

- I'm wondering if you could work on making dispassionate, sound decisions from now on.

- You have a great deal of talent, but sometimes that gets lost when you fail to use good judgment.

- After the spate of bad decisions you've made, I have to call your judgment into question.

- I have to judge you because you're incapable of judging yourself, or anything else for that matter.

- Unfortunately you seem unable to discern the proper course of action in every situation.

- Your lack of good judgment and discernment make me worry about the future of this department.

- It seems that I am the one who has exhibited a lack of discernment—by hiring you.

- How could I rate you high on discernment? You couldn't even figure out what this meeting was about.

Harsh

Appraise an Employee's Creativity

Glowing

- You always impress me with your ability to think outside the box.

- You have one of the most creative, original minds I've ever had the pleasure of meeting.

- You are one of the most creative employees we've ever had–keep up the good work!

- There is no one on staff with a better track record of creative achievement than you.

- Not only are you creative, but you've worked hard to put that innate talent to good use.

- Your creativity and ingenuity are what keep this department going.

- We are lucky to have someone as talented and creative as you on staff.

- Your approach is sometimes a bit unconventional, but that goes with a territory with creative people.

- You are creative, but sometimes I wish you would step even further outside of the box.

- Sometimes I feel as though you don't allow your creative talents to really shine.

- I can tell that you are trying, but the creative "spark" just isn't there most of the time.

- I know you are doing your best to be creative, which is what has me concerned.

- Your creative efforts are pedestrian and commonplace. You really need to up the ante.

- You're either creative or you're not; unfortunately I don't think you are.

Harsh

- You have many talents, but being creative is not one of them.

- I wonder if you would be more comfortable in a less creative field.

- We need to find you some work that doesn't involve thinking creatively.

- You don't have a creative bone in your body, do you?

Appraise an Employee's Problem-Solving Skills

Glowing

- I admire how you've been able to think up a solution to every problem that crops up.

- You have an uncanny ability to always bring about the proper outcome, even under duress.

- You handled the problems we had last year with insight, good judgment, and aplomb.

- When I need someone to take on a big problem, I need only look to you.

- I have no problem with the way you've addressed problems in the department so far.

- You certainly give every problem your best effort, but I think we need to raise the bar just a bit.

- Fortunately, even though you stumbled a bit, all of our problems this year worked themselves out.

- This isn't about the problems themselves, but how you deal with them.

- I wish I could give you A's for your problem-solving skills, but in all good conscience, I can't.

Critical

- Your troubleshooting skills could really use some brushing up. How can we make that happen?

- I handle the most difficult problems here, so I'm unsure why you're foundering so badly.

- It's not about merely starting to fix something; it's actually fixing it that is most important.

- Even the tiniest problem evokes panic and flailing on your part. What gives?

- You seem ready to abandon ship as soon as there's an iceberg.

- I'm not sure that I can trust you to address even the smallest problem in the department anymore.

- Rather than solve our problems, you only seem to add to them.

- The last thing I need is more problems; I think we need to rethink your employment here.

How to Appraise an Employee's Product Knowledge

Praising

- Your product knowledge is exhaustive and virtually encyclopedic.

- You are as familiar with our products as I am with the back of my hand.

- Your product knowledge is legendary around here.

- There's nothing you don't know about our products, is there?

- Your exhaustive and comprehensive product knowledge is what has allowed you to succeed.

- It didn't take you very long at all to familiarize yourself with our products, did it?

- I have tried time and again, but I can't poke holes in your product knowledge. Impressive!

- With more work, I know you'll be able to get an even better handle on what it is we do here.

- Your excellence as an employee all comes down to knowing what it is you're creating here.

- You don't know everything about our products, but I can see that you are trying hard to learn.

- Your product knowledge has a few gaps that need to be filled in order for you to do well here.

- There's no substitute for a solid knowledge of our products; I suggest that you study up before your next review.

- Our excellent products won't do anyone any good if you don't even know what they are.

- You don't seem very motivated to understand our products. Why is that?

- Have we not given you the tools you need to learn about what we create here?

- If product knowledge is king, then you would have to be a pauper, I'm afraid.

- If you don't demonstrate a thorough understanding of our products by your next review, we'll need to take other steps.

- An employee with such a limited—no, nonexistent—understanding of our company's offerings is essentially useless.

Critical

How to Appraise an Employee's Research Skills

Glowing

- No one on our team digs as deeply or as thoroughly into a topic as you do.

- Nobody is as good as getting even the most obscure facts straight on every single subject.

- When I need unimpeachable research I know I can always count on you to come through.

- No one is as able to research relevant topics with more breadth and depth than you.

- You have the uncanny ability to ferret out every single fact about the topic or issue at hand.

- Most people can research a topic adequately, but your research is notable for its thoroughness.

- I could not have completed this research project without the work you've done.

- You've gone above and beyond what I expected as a researcher. Good job.

- I have no problem giving you more research in the future, as you haven't let me down yet.

- Your research is passable, but it seems somewhat lacking in breadth and depth.

- Researching is a complex but necessary part of the job, so I'm willing to help you learn.

- You seem a bit out of your depth when it comes to researching topics for me. Why is that?

- Did you never have to do a research paper in college?

- Anyone can learn how to do research, but you need to be willing to put in some time and effort.

Critical

- Unfortunately, your research only scrapes the surface. You need to dig much deeper if you're going to make it here.

- What will it take for us to bring your research skills up to speed?

- Research is a learned skill. All you've demonstrated so far is that you have a lot more to learn.

- Real research involves a lot more than just performing a perfunctory Google search.

- Really, with a researcher as untrained as you on staff, I'm better off just remaining ignorant.

- I have only one word to describe your research this past year: useless.

How to Appraise an Employee's Troubleshooting Skills

Glowing

- You always manage to cut through all the extraneous details to get to the heart of a problem.

- When I look up the word *troubleshooter* in the dictionary, I see your name.

- When we encounter a snarl at work, I know I can always count on you to make sense of it all.

- Snafus are a part of the job, but they are no match for your peerless troubleshooting skills.

- I always know who to call when we encounter those seemingly intractable problems.

- When I need someone to take on a bad situation, you are my go-to guy.

- We like to call you "the Cleaner" because you make bad problems disappear.

- I feel confident that you can handle virtually any problem that comes your way.

- While you've never actually solved any problems, your calming influence has been helpful.

- If you learned how to troubleshoot, it would make you that much more valuable as an employee.

- A smooth sea never made a skilled mariner. It's time to be the skilled mariner I know you are.

- You're very bright, but the way you approach problems is not always the most productive or helpful.

- I know you mean well, but sometimes I get the feeling that you give up before you even try.

- You do your best, but unfortunately, your best has never really helped us figure anything out.

- You don't really seem to have the ability to calmly and logically troubleshoot sticky situations.

- Every job has its problems and difficulties; it's how you respond to them that counts.

- Unfortunately, your lack of engagement in our problems has forced me to step in and solve most of them myself.

- I don't expect you to single-handedly solve every problem, but I do expect you to at least take a stab at it.

- You seem to add to our problems instead of solving them.

- There is no reason to rank your troubleshooting skills, as I have yet to see you demonstrate any.

- You couldn't unkink a Slinky, so why would I trust you to troubleshoot something that really matters?

Critical

How to Appraise an Employee's Overall Work Quality

Glowing

- There simply aren't enough superlatives in the dictionary to describe the quality of your work.

- When I stack your work against that of your peers, they don't even show up on the radar.

- You have single-handedly raised the bar here on overall work quality.

- You have put everyone else who has held your position to shame.

- Your work here is, and always has been, peerless and without reproach.

- I can't think of anyone else here who does work that's as good as yours.

- Your work here has been consistently flawless. How do you do it?

- The quality of your work makes you a credit to this organization.

- You definitely set the standard for excellence on our team.

- I have never, ever, seen anyone perform at such a high level.

- I doubt that anyone will ever surpass the quality of your work here.

- Your work here has been consistently good and steady. Just keep it up!

- In general I think your work has been of good quality, but I see some areas that could use improvement.

- Let me ask you: How do *you* feel the quality of your work has been?

- Sometimes being good is good enough, but I would like to see you try a bit harder.

- You work hard; that's obvious, but the quality of your work isn't always where it should be.

- You seem to be missing the mark more often than you are hitting it lately. What's going on?

- I'm not feeling all that good about your work, so how could you possibly be feeling good about it?

- If your work doesn't improve soon, we may need to rethink your role in this department.

- This company has no room for mediocrity, let alone poor quality work. Please think about that.

- I don't believe I have seen a spottier work record than yours. You really need to step it up.

- It is unfair to the other workers that they continually have to pick up your slack.

- At least you are consistent: you *always* let us down.

Critical

How to Appraise an Employee's Potential for Promotion

Praising

- We are going to run out of new projects for you long before you run out of the potential to take them on.

- Why even bother denying it: someday you'll be running this place.

- If you continue on this trajectory of excellence, the company—no, the world—will be your oyster.

- You are the kind of person who is destined to go places, including *way* up the corporate ladder.

- You've already impressed leadership as someone who will go very far, indeed.

- If you set your sights on climbing the corporate hierarchy, I will be your most ardent supporter.

- I know we are going to see great things from you someday, as long as you apply yourself.

- I think a promotion will be in the cards for you someday, assuming that you make it happen.

- You've shown us some good work, but you'll need to up the ante if you want to get promoted.

- You have a great deal of potential but seemingly little drive to realize that potential.

- I never believe in holding an employee back—unless it's deserved.

- I think you would be quite content if you stayed in this position forever. Would you agree with that?

- Not everyone is destined for higher things. *All* work has dignity, after all.

Critical

- You seem to value playing it safe more than you want to rise in the ranks. Why is that?

- I think you lack the drive and determination to rise up the ranks. But please prove me wrong!

- Give your work quality, it's difficult to determine exactly when we'll be able to promote you, if ever.

- Most of the time promotions are given when they are earned.

- I don't advocate promoting just to promote. You need to do something to actually deserve it.

- You seem very happily ensconced in the status quo. Tell me why I should change that.

- I think you've gone as far as you can in this company. Maybe you should start expanding your horizons.

How to Appraise an Employee's Selling Skills

Praising

- You are without a doubt the most capable, competent, and successful salesperson we've ever had.

- You consistently bring in the biggest accounts and the best numbers. Well done!

- I don't know how you do it, but your numbers are consistently the highest of anyone's here.

- You are the role model for all the other salespeople in the department.

- I can't praise your sales performance highly enough. Keep up the good work!

- You talked a big sales game when you started here; you've accomplished all that and more.

- I don't have to tell you that your numbers were quite good this year, as always.

- I have nothing overtly bad to say about your performance this year. It's been adequate.

- Your sales skills could use some brushing up; perhaps we should go over the manual again.

- I have high hopes for your numbers next quarter; I hope you prove me right.

- Your sales skills are uneven at best. Where do think you could use the most help?

- You really need to brush up on your ABC's of sales: *Always Be Closing.*

- Look, you're a gregarious guy, but you seem to lack the temerity to bring in the big accounts.

- I hired you because I thought you had the skills necessary to bring in the numbers. What happened?

- I'll give you a pass this quarter, but next quarter you need to buckle down and make it happen.

- I know you can sell, but neither I nor the company can wait forever for you to prove yourself.

- When we sketched out your sales goals, I never imagined that you would fall so short.

- You are nowhere near as strong a seller as I had thought.

- Whenever you decide to actually apply yourself to selling our products, let me know.

- Maybe sales isn't the career you should have chosen.

Critical

How to Appraise an Employee's Customer-Service Skills

Praising

- You always seem to know exactly what to do to retain our existing customers and gain new ones.

- You are the model for how excellent customer service should look in action.

- You have an innate grasp of customer service and the skills and experience to match.

- No one else has the customer-service skills that you have.

- You have really raised the bar here on how we treat our customers.

- No one gets better treatment than our customers, and this is primarily attributable to your efforts.

- The fact that our customers are so happy shows just how much you care about great service.

- The only reason I'm not giving you a higher score for customer service is that the rating scale only goes up to 10.

- Whenever I want to provide great customer service, I think of what you do and try to emulate it.

- No one is as good as you at handling our customer's needs. You're simply the best.

- Customer service is something anyone can do well if they just make an effort.

- In general, I have no complaints with how you handle and serve our customers.

- I'd like to see you do more in terms of really going the extra mile to make our customers happy.

- Your skills in dealing with customers could use some polishing.

- The way you deal with our customers has been a bit of a concern for me.

- If you can't give customers the service they desire, someone else will. Just remember that.

- No customer would want to deal with someone who obviously cares so little about service.

- I think we need to go back to the drawing board and redefine what the word *service* means.

- You don't seem comfortable or adept in dealing with customers; maybe we need to rethink your job description.

- I simply can't have you ruining our reputation for excellent service.

Critical

Part 3
Interpersonal Skills

Interpersonal skills are arguably one of the most important factors in the success–or failure–of any career or company. A lack of them can impede or even completely derail the career of even the most talented employee, so always make sure you cover this in your reviews.

"Interpersonal skills" as a competency is a large umbrella, but this is by design. There is no real way to measure these skills by using metrics; therefore, evaluating them is a subjective process. For example, how do you measure just how friendly someone is? This is an area where you'll need to be careful to avoid letting your personal prejudices and past history unduly affect your opinions and how you couch things.

Sometimes it's also a good idea to have the consensus of other managers in the department or company. If an employee is unfriendly with everyone, not just you or your customers, you'll have a more solid case to build when it comes time for performance reviews and evaluations.

How to Appraise an Employee's Ability to Work With a Team

Glowing

- Your colleagues' opinion says it all: you're a beloved and valued member of this team.

- Rarely do you meet someone who works well both autonomously and as part of a team.

- You're doing so well in your group projects that your teammates have voted you MVP.

- I can't believe how well you've integrated with the team.

- The fact that your teammates think so highly of you says a lot.

- You are not just a cog in the wheel; you're an integral part of your team's success. Nice work!

- You seem generally okay with the team projects, but not overly enthusiastic.

- From what I can see, you seem to work pretty well with others.

- I think you need to work a bit harder on playing well with others.

- I must say that your teamwork skills are a little rough around the edges.

- You seem much more comfortable working solo; is there a reason for this?

- Your teammates want you to succeed, too, but you aren't working *with* them.

- I think you and your team could do great things together, if you just worked on your flexibility and humility a bit.

- Your work style is alienating the other team members. Haven't you noticed?

Critical

- You seem very out of sync with the way your team operates. How can we address that?

- I really doubt that you have what it takes to work well with others. But please prove me wrong!

- If you can't subjugate your agenda for the greater good of the team, you'll be dead in the water.

- Someone like you is probably incapable of working with others.

- Just because there is no I in team, doesn't mean that group projects are personally unfulfilling.

- Unless you are willing to play well with the others, we'll need to think about reassigning you elsewhere.

How to Appraise an Employee's Ability to Work Solo

Praising

- One may be the loneliest number for most, but for you, it spells productivity.

- I admire how you are really able to focus and get things done all on your own.

- I appreciate that I never have to watch or check up on you to make sure you're being productive.

- Your discipline as a self-starter has been invaluable in your success here.

- It takes a special sort of person who is disciplined and focused enough to work solo.

- I must say I am thrilled with how you've taken the initiative here, all by yourself.

- I admire an employee who knows exactly what to do without others breathing down his neck.

- You really seem to shine when you are able to go off by yourself and focus.

- Not many people could stand to work solo all the time. You're to be commended.

- I really appreciate the way you take the bull by the horns and run with it, all by yourself.

- I was pleasantly surprised to see you step up and take responsibility; I'd like to see more of that.

- I trust your ability to handle the job, but I would like to see more independence of thought.

- I don't mind if you work by yourself all the time as long as everything gets done.

- You need to rely less on others and more on your own initiative and strengths.

- So much of our company's success is based on everyone shouldering their own burden.

- It seems hard for you to work well without a lot of input or guidance from others. Would you agree?

- I think you need to get more comfortable venturing out on your own every now and then.

- If you want something done right, you should consider doing it yourself.

- I was hoping you could take on tasks without any help, but obviously my hope was unfounded.

- You can't have someone there to hold your hand all the time, you know.

- If you were a rookie I could understand a little hand-holding, but it's time to cut the apron strings.

- If you can't go it alone, perhaps I need to look into finding someone who is comfortable with that.

Critical

How to Appraise an Employee's Ability to Communicate Effectively

Glowing

- You set the standard here for how to communicate clearly, efficiently, and respectfully.

- Everyone always appreciates your clear and respectful communication style.

- You have a way of clearing things up and helping everyone get on the same page.

- I wish everyone were as good a communicator as you are.

- Ronald Regan, the Great Communicator, had nothing on you! [*joking*]

- Communicating with you is always a pleasure; you make even the difficult topics easy to discuss.

- In general, I think you do a good job of getting your message across.

- You are always clear on the facts, but sometimes your delivery is wanting.

- It's not always clear what you want or what you are thinking. What can we do to address this?

- I think your communication style can be a bit confusing and even upsetting to some. Can we work on that?

- It seems that you expect everyone to read your mind, but that is *not* the path to clarity or productivity.

- Our goal in communicating is not to obfuscate matters, but to make them clearer for all concerned.

Critical

- People shouldn't have to struggle to make sense of what you are saying.

- The department won't function unless everyone is on the same page. How can we make this happen?

- Do you enjoy being inscrutable or unreadable? Most people don't respond to that.

- Hoarding information in that manner will get you nowhere fast.

- Communicating with you is akin to using two cans and a piece of string as a phone.

How to Appraise an Employee's Friendliness

Praising

- Your friendliness and good nature are the fulcrum upon which this department turns.

- You are, hands down, the friendliest and easiest-to-work-with employee I've ever had.

- Your natural friendliness and appreciation of people is a huge asset to this department.

- Nobody ever has a bad thing to say about you; how do you do it?

- Your agreeableness is what makes you so easy to work with.

- Because you're so friendly on the job, people naturally gravitate to you.

- I wouldn't say you're crazy-happy, but you're certainly pleasant to most people.

- There is genuine kindness and then there's fake friendly. We need more of the former.

- I think you could make more of an effort to be friendlier to your colleagues.

- Sometimes your occasional moodiness makes it difficult to work with you.

- Being friendly is not part of your job description, but it might help you get along better with others.

- Why are you so angry all the time? It doesn't take much effort to put in a friendly word every now and then.

- I'm not saying you need to be sickeningly cheerful; just try and be bearable, is all I'm asking.

- Sure, you're productive, but why do you have to be so unfriendly to everyone in the process?

- Your unfriendly demeanor is starting to cause problems in the department.

- If you were any grouchier, we'd have to find you a garbage can to call home. [*joking*]

- I can't order you to be friendly, but I can ask that you not bite the head off of everyone you meet.

- Your perpetual foul mood is really starting to affect morale.

- You've now succeeded in alienating not only me but your entire department.

- I would tell you to turn your frown upside down, but I'm afraid you'd turn on *me*. [*joking/sarcastic*]

Critical

How to Appraise an Employee's Effect on Morale

Praising

- You have single-handedly summoned the troops and encouraged everyone in the process.

- Because of you, this department is humming along more productively and happily than ever before.

- When you're around, everything just seems more "up" and productive.

- You have this amazing way of bringing out the best in others while keeping them happy.

- Morale has never been higher since you came aboard. Just keep up whatever it is you're doing.

- Your good influence is one of the reasons your department is such a happy place.

- I appreciate your recent efforts to perk things up; it's been a refreshing change.

- I know you've been swimming against the current of the naysayers, but don't give up just yet.

- Good morale is an integral component of productivity. I know you want to be on the positive side of that equation.

- While most of the time your presence is appreciated, sometimes people feel as though you are bringing them down.

- Complaints are an opportunity to make things better, but how you voice them is very important.

- I know you think you're just being a realist, but the negativity is handicapping your team.

- It only takes one bad apple to spoil the lot—do you really want to be that bad apple?

Critical

- Based on the current state of morale, you may need an attitude adjustment.

- What is it about this place or these people that you hate so much?

- I take no pleasure in saying this, but your attitude is ruining everything that was once good here.

- Your negativity and woe-is-me approach flies in the face of all the good energy I've put into this company.

- It is as if you mean to take everyone down a notch just for fun. Why is that?

- Do you take pleasure in making people miserable?

- A cancer that has started to invade the surrounding tissues needs to be excised. Do you understand what I'm saying?

How to Appraise an Employee's Workspace/Personal Space

Praising

- Your workspace deserves to be featured in *House Beautiful.*

- Your workspace is a model of productivity and attention to aesthetics.

- Your workspace truly is a reflection of who you are: neat, organized, fun, and creative.

- If everyone put the same effort into their workspace decor, this office would be a very pleasant place, indeed.

- Your decorative efforts have lifted the spirits of everyone around you. Well done!

- If we all put as much effort into our work as you do into your surroundings, we'd be in business.

- Some people attach no importance to their surroundings, but I think that's a mistake.

- We spend most of our waking life here; it might as well be a homey and inviting place!

- I know you mean well, but your enthusiasm for interior design needs to be toned down a bit.

- You've obviously invested a lot in decorating your workspace; maybe try and tone it down a bit.

- Personal expression is one thing, but please keep your workspace professional and appropriate.

- Everyone's desk is a personal statement, but I'm unsure what kind of statement you're trying to make.

- When I sit down at your desk it feels like I've settled into an alternate, somewhat disquieting reality.

- Perhaps we should think about hiring a corporate stylist or interior designer.

- While we encourage creativity and freedom of expression, it needs to stay within the bounds of professionalism.

- You really need to take more pride in your workspace and surroundings.

- Do you perhaps dump all your garbage into your office?

- Your desk is such an eyesore, we're afraid to let clients come in lest they see it.

- If you don't clean up this unholy mess, we'll need to send in the crew from *Buried Alive*. [*joking*]

Critical

How to Appraise an Employee's Grooming/Dress/Hygiene

Glowing

- You're always so well-dressed, you look as though you stepped right off the runway.

- You are always perfectly turned out, no matter the occasion; what's your secret?

- You've really set the bar high when it comes to attire and personal grooming.

- You always look so great and pulled together; you even put the CEO to shame!

- You make it easy to look professional and appropriate in every situation.

- Sometimes you don't look like your normal, pulled-together self, but that happens to the best of us.

- When you look good and smell good, you just feel good—don't you agree?

- Appearance counts no matter what industry you're in; perhaps we need to go over our expectations in that regard.

- As you bump up the personal grooming a notch, you'll find that more opportunities will open up here.

- Being well-dressed and well-groomed is really just basic politeness in close quarters.

- Some days you look as though you slept in your car; is everything okay?

- Know that good grooming is an integral part of being well-turned-out—and successful.

Critical

- We are all professionals here and should conduct ourselves accordingly: with pride, attention to grooming and dress, and the self-confidence to match.

- Some people, including clients, have started to complain about your lack of personal grooming.

- If you want to move up the totem pole, you should look into a more professional appearance.

- Good grooming is just basic human life skills. Or did you not learn that in grade school?

- They always say to dress for the job you want; in your case it looks as though you'd prefer to be a janitor. [joking]

When an Employee Foments Conflict

Subtle

- Maybe it would be better if you kept your honest thoughts to yourself sometimes.

- The only thing worse than constant conflict is groupthink; at least we don't have the latter.

- I know you mean well, but sometimes you rub people the wrong way.

- I would appreciate more of an effort in picking up the slack instead of always stirring the pot.

- You have so much potential, but you seem to attract conflict wherever you go.

- People seem to have a hard time getting along when you're around; why is that?

- Pitting people against each other is something only amateurs do when they are insecure.

- Causing conflict within the ranks is not something I will tolerate.

- It's not necessary to fight with every single person who disagrees with you.

- I've decided that we can't have all this conflict without resolution. That part is up to you.

- I think you need to start over and come from a place of mutual care, respect, and cocreation.

- You seem to take pride in creating drama and causing conflict—not something I'm interested in fostering.

- Yes, you can't make an omelet without breaking a few eggs, but to me that's just a cop-out.

- I'm not asking for groupthink; just mutual respect and room for everyone's ideas.

- While a certain amount of conflict is good for a team, I think you crossed the line long ago.

- You've certainly established a monopoly on corporate infighting, haven't you?

- Without question you're the most combative person I have ever had on my team.

- I believe if I just fired you now, the infighting would stop completely. What do you think?

Harsh

When an Employee Oversteps Boundaries

Subtle

- The concept of boundaries means that certain things are yours, and certain things belong to others.

- I believe that every employee has a place, and that there is a place for every employee.

- Everything here works better when everyone is taking care of their own stuff.

- Chaos results when everyone is running around doing things they shouldn't be doing.

- It's important that everyone here be responsible for their own duties.

- While I appreciate your go-getter attitude, let's try not to step on any toes, okay?

- I can see that you want to help. Just be careful not to trespass into anyone else's territory.

- I know you're only trying to help, but you are alienating people by trying to do their jobs.

- You're not going to make any friends by nosing your way into others' responsibilities.

- Once you've handled your own duties, you still need clearance before tackling someone else's.

- The next time I catch you doing someone's work I'll need to write you up.

- How can I run a department when I'm not sure who is doing what?

- There are times to butt into someone else's business, but this really isn't one of them.

Harsh

- If you continue to overstep your responsibilities, we'll need to rethink your job description.

- Careful: you invade the territories of others at your own peril.

- People are now perceiving you as a suck-up and brownnoser; is that what you want?

- If you have designs on others' jobs, it would better if you just came out and said so.

- I have a feeling that if we went into a revolving door together, you'd come out ahead. [*sarcastic*]

When an Employee Complains Excessively

Subtle

- While I appreciate the fact that you care, it's important not to be a constant downer.

- Complaints are necessary, but you need to be really careful how you voice them.

- For each complaint you bring to my door, I'd like you to come up with three possible solutions.

- A complaint is an opportunity to make things better, but in your case that's all we ever hear.

- You are becoming a source of discontent and low morale—is that what you want?

- Employees who whine all the time usually don't climb very high in the organization.

- I can understand a little whining every now and then, but you never, ever, stop.

- You're far too talented at what you do to be labeled a complainer.

Punitive

- Don't bother me with these trifles; you need to grow up and figure stuff out yourself.

- Nobody wants to hang around or work with a noisy negativist.

- We've had complainers around here before. They usually just give up and go away.

- Just think how much more productive you could be if you didn't complain so much.

- You're introducing a lot of negative energy into the department and I don't like it.

- You're a fine case of whine, alright.

- How do I know you're complaining? Your mouth is moving.

- You're like the boy who cried wolf: eventually people will just start to ignore you.

When an Employee Brownnoses

Subtle

- I value your opinion greatly, especially when you're willing to contradict me.

- I appreciate your enthusiasm, but you really don't need to go out of your way to flatter me.

- I know you mean well, but sometimes your slavish devotion comes across as disingenuous.

- I am more interested in hearing the opinions of people who are willing to risk my displeasure.

- I like to treat all of my colleagues as equals, and I think you should, too.

- Agreeing with me all the time isn't going to get you anywhere.

- Nobody respects a sycophant.

- I don't want toadies or flatterers on my staff; I want people who are willing to speak their mind.

- I am very aware of what you are doing and it won't work, I can assure you.

- Rather than flattering me, I'd prefer to see you putting more energy into your work.

- Flattering well is a real art, but so far you haven't shown that you have any talent for it.

- Please disagree with me every now and then so that I know you're not my shadow. [*joking*]

- The inveterate brown-noser is the very antithesis of a true professional, just so you know.

- Believe me, I don't brownnose, and don't encourage you to do it, either.

- I've got a pretty good brownnosing detector and you're lighting it up right now.

- If this is your best tactic for moving up the ladder, you'll need to step it up. [*sarcasm*]

Harsh

When an Employee Socializes Excessively at Work

Understanding

- It's fine to have a good time here, but let's keep it within reason.

- I'm as guilty as anyone of wasting time at work, but I know that I can't spend hours doing so.

- It's great that you get along so well with everyone; just don't let it affect your productivity.

- I know it's fun hanging out with your coworkers. Just make sure that everything gets done.

- Later you'll wish you could get back the hours of time you wasted socializing.

- I am so glad that we all have fun here; just please try and stay focused on work, okay?

- You can spend a half hour hanging out with everyone in the morning, but then it's back to work.

- I don't want to be a wet blanket, but you really need to buckle down and get some work done.

- I really wish you could apply yourself as readily to work as you do to your socializing.

- There is a time and a place for everything, and this is the place and time for work.

- With all the chatting you do I'm amazed that you get any work done at all!

- Yes, you are having fun, but where is my ROI (return on investment) from this?

- If you can't stop all the socializing, I'm afraid I'll have to write you up.

- While the excess chatting may seem innocent, it's starting to affect productivity negatively.

- What you are doing is actually costing the company money.

- How could you possibly think that we would pay you to goof off with your friends?

- If you can't keep yourself focused on work, I'll see to it that you no longer have any work.

Punitive

When Two Employees Are Romantically Involved

Permissive

- I know you are attracted to each other, but I am concerned about the potential effect on your work.

- I have a "don't ask, don't tell" policy when it comes to my employees' romantic lives.

- As long as you keep the PDA (public displays of affection) under wraps, I could care less.

- I have no problem with the relationship, as long as you both disclose it to HR.

- I don't care what you do in your private time as long as the work gets done.

- This may be a blessing in disguise since neither of you really has much of a private life.

- I'm indifferent to this kind of thing, as long as you don't let it affect your work.

- That's fine, but what if you break up? That could be uncomfortable for everyone.

- Are you sure you want to do this? Workplace romances can be unpredictable.

- Please, take a few moments to consider the potential ramifications of a romance on the job.

- You need to ask yourself if this is really a good idea for either of you, or for the team as a whole.

- I see this only as a potential distraction from the real reason we're all here.

- Haven't you ever heard the phrase: "Don't get your honey where you make your money"?

Punitive

- The minute I see anyone's work suffering, I'll report this to HR without any hesitation.

- This is clearly a violation of company policy. I am going to need to write up both of you.

- Some companies merely discourage workplace romances, but I'm here to tell you that it won't happen on my watch.

When an Employee Gossips

Lax

- There is no problem with gossiping on the job, as long as it's all true! [*joking*]

- I don't mind if you gossip, as long as you keep me in the loop. [*joking*]

- I don't care about gossip on the job as long as it's not about me! [*joking*]

- I enjoy a juicy morsel as much as the next person; just try not to let this affect your work.

- We all have a taste for gossip, but it really needs to be kept in check during work hours.

- Spreading rumors will only affect productivity negatively, and I know you don't want that.

- I find myself wanting gossip every now and then, but stop myself. I hope you can, too.

- How would you feel if someone talked about you behind your back like that?

- What goes on at the watercooler should stay at the watercooler.

- Do realize how those kind of comments can hurt other people?

Punitive

- I have a hard time believing that you don't know how vile those remarks are.

- The funny thing about gossip is that it often comes back to haunt you.

- Gossiping and spreading rumors will only have a negative effect on your career.

- I'm only going to tell you once: don't gossip about your coworkers.

- We have a no-tolerance policy for gossip here.

- The hatemongering and rumor mill have got to stop; otherwise I will have to write you up.

- People don't respect or trust someone who trades in rumors. That's just good judgment.

- Your teammates don't deserve that kind of treatment. Keep it up and you'll be gone.

Part 4

Attitude

Attitude is another one of those "soft," subjective skills that can have a huge and potentially negative effect on your bottom line. That's why it's important to always stick to the facts. Saying, "You made three negative comments during the last meeting," is better than saying, "You bring morale down around here." *Just the facts, ma'am!*

Herb Kelleher of Southwest Airlines had a saying: "Hire for attitude; train for skill." That's because he realized just how important attitude was in his employees, from the people who cleaned the bathrooms to the pilots who flew the planes. Attitude is the springboard from which everything else happens in your department. How are your employees affecting morale? How well do they fit into the company culture and hierarchy? How disciplined are they? How open are they to negative feedback?

Remember that good attitude is contagious. Be the change you want to see in your employees, and I can almost guarantee that they will follow suit.

Appraise an Employee's Overall Attitude

Praising

- You are one of the most positive, upbeat employees I've ever had.

- Everyone here really appreciates your optimism and can-do attitude.

- Your ability to maintain a positive attitude, even in the face of challenges, is to be commended.

- I wish everyone around here had your winning attitude. What's your secret?

- Your positive attitude is a breath of fresh air. Keep it up!

- In general, you seem to bring a fairly positive attitude to your work.

- I think you would find this job much more rewarding if you approached it with a better attitude.

- Life is 10 percent what happens to you, and 90 percent attitude. This job is no different.

- I'm not asking you to be over-the-top happy all the time; just a more positive approach would be great.

- You work hard and contribute a great deal, but sometimes you are a bit of a downer to be around.

- I'd rather have a positive person working for me who doesn't contribute much, than a noisy negativist who does it all.

- Sometimes I think you could use a bit of an attitude adjustment.

Critical

- I am concerned that your poor attitude is starting to rub off on the others. How can we fix that?

- Is there a reason why you have such a negative attitude all the time? Are you unhappy here?

- You don't have to be happy all the time. Just try to put on a happy face to keep up morale.

- Look, your attitude is abysmal. You either pick it up or we'll need to revisit your role here.

- You make the Grinch look like Mr. Rogers.

Appraise an Employee's Initiative

Praising

- I know I never have to prod you to take care of things. Your initiative is to be commended.

- I always wanted a self-starter like you on my staff. Nice work!

- No one else here has even a tenth of your initiative.

- The great thing about you is that you always spot a need before anyone else does.

- Your initiative is about on par with everyone else's here. I have no complaints.

- You seem to take initiative on most projects but I'd like to see more of that.

- Sometimes I feel as though you fail to take initiative when it really counts. How can we fix this?

- I need to be able to trust you to take care of things, especially when I'm not here to watch you.

Critical

- The last thing I need is an employee whose hand I need to hold the entire day.

- If I have to wait for you to finally take some initiative, this department may just grind to a halt.

- Your record on taking initiative is pretty abysmal. This needs to be fixed, and fast.

- If I have to goad you into actually doing your work, there's really no sense in your working here at all.

- I really don't have time or inclination to baby-sit someone who can't get his act together.

Appraise an Employee's Focus

Praising

- Your ability to stay focused no matter what is going on around you is commendable.

- Sometimes I think you're almost too focused on your work. [joking]

- Your focus is so laser-sharp, I'm afraid you just might burn a hole through your desk! [joking]

- I've never had an employee with the ability to maintain such intense focus until the job is done.

- I have no complaints regarding your ability to remain focused and attentive on the job.

- Without an ability to stay focused and on-task all the time, your talents will just go to waste.

- You seem a bit scattered sometimes. Is there anything I can do to help with this?

- I'd like to see more focus and attention coming from you in the months ahead.

Critical

- I don't think you focus as well or as consistently as you could. What do you think?

- Staring off into space and constantly checking your watch will not get you very far here.

- I'm no longer convinced that you have the ability to remain focused and do this job.

- Your lack of focus around here is driving me and all of your coworkers to distraction.

- You seem to have no problem directing your attention to the video games on your computer.

- Sometimes I think you may have ADHD or something; have you looked into that?

Appraise an Employee's Dedication

Praising

- I have never had an employee as dedicated to making the company succeed as you.

- You are the model of dedication and commitment to this company.

- If you were any more dedicated to this job, you'd probably sleep here. [joking]

- You are by the far the most dedicated employee I've ever had the pleasure to work with.

- Your dedication to this job is unimpeachable and to be commended.

- You set the bar very high here, with your dedication to your work and to the company.

- You are here when I arrive in the morning and the last person to leave at night. You put me to shame! [joking]

Critical

- You obviously take this job, and your loyalty to this company, very seriously. I really appreciate that.

- Yes, you are dedicated, but you need to work smarter, not necessarily harder.

- I know you feel as though you are dedicated, but I'd like to see that evidenced often in your actions.

- While you are skilled and talented, I question whether you truly are as dedicated as you could be.

- Without dedication, all of your efforts here will just come to naught.

- You don't seem to take your job very seriously at all. Can you tell me why that is?

- Most days you show up just to collect your pay-check. There's not a lot of dedication that I can see.

- You'll need to really up the ante when it comes to dedication if you want to excel here.

- I find your lack of dedication...disturbing.

Appraise an Employee's Professionalism

Praising

- I've never seen you act in any way that wasn't completely correct and professional.

- You have the impeccable, unflagging professionalism of someone who is destined for great things.

- You are the very embodiment of professionalism in everything you do. Excellent work!

- I wish I had been as professional at your age. I'd be in the corner office right now.

- The office culture has become more professional since you've joined us, and I have you to thank.

- This is a job for a professional, and you've certainly demonstrated that you are just that.

- With just a few lapses here and there, you conduct yourself in a fairly professional manner.

- You can't be too professional on my watch.

- If you bumped up the professionalism a bit, I think you'd be surprised at the doors that would open.

- Your lapses in professionalism are casting a doubtful light on your otherwise excellent performance.

- There is really no excuse for not conducting yourself like a professional at all times.

- Your lack of professionalism really has me concerned. How can we address this?

- People have been complaining about your unprofessional behavior. Care to comment on that?

- The janitor who comes here on the weekends is more of a pro than you are.

- Professionalism is a learned trait, but unfortunately you don't seem to have picked up on it at all.

- You're a loose cannon with your complete disregard for professionalism. I can't have that.

Critical

Appraise an Employee's Tact/Diplomacy

Praising

- You are the very model of tact and diplomacy in all that you do.

- I know I can always count on you for your supreme sense of tact and diplomacy.

- Your diplomacy is one of the reasons why we've done so well this year. Keep it up!

- You show real emotional intelligence in the way you always exhibit great tact and diplomacy.

- It's a blessing to have someone around here who doesn't act like a teenager in a food fight.

- Aside from a few lapses in discretion, your behavior is, in general, fairly tactful and diplomatic.

- A little more tact and attention to diplomacy would suit you better.

- I think you may need to learn a bit more about how to be diplomatic in all situations.

- Your tactless behavior on the job has alienated several people, including me.

- Sometimes you seem more like a bull in a china shop, the way you just mow people over with your lack of tact.

Critical

Appraise an Employee's Self-Confidence

Praising

- I admire your complete and unwavering confidence in yourself.

- My confidence in you is only exceeded by how confident you are in your own skills.

- There are some people who have a right to be a little arrogant, and you are one of them.

- Your self-confidence is one of the reasons I believe so strongly in you.

- Your confidence in yourself makes everyone around you feel confident, too.

- This kind of self-confidence and comfort in one's own skin is a rarity these days.

- Your self-confidence in the face of opposition is what makes you a real winner.

- Don't be so shy: let your self-confidence shine for all to see!

- You shouldn't let challenges rattle you so much; you have every reason to believe in yourself.

- Sometimes I get the feeling that you don't believe in yourself as much as you ought to.

- You get so down on yourself that it actually hampers your productivity here.

- All the great ideas in the world are useless without the confidence to act on them.

- As far as self-confidence goes, I always say, "Fake it until you make it."

- If you don't believe in yourself, why should I, or anyone else for that matter?

Critical

Appraise an Employee's Energy

Praising

- You are, without fail, indefatigable and relentless, even when the chips are down.

- There's no doubt in my mind that your energy will propel you to ever greater heights.

- You're just a firecracker in action, aren't you?

- Before I met you I thought it was impossible to be "on" 24/7. Now I know I was wrong.

- You are a perpetual motion machine around here. That kind of energy is a real gift.

- You seem to have more energy than the Eveready Bunny! [*joking*]

- You never, ever seem to run out of steam—how do you do it?

- It makes me tired just watching you in action. [*joking*]

- You have the energy and drive of at least five people put together.

- Your energy, vigor, and liveliness in the face of struggle make you a very valuable employee.

- I admire your energy; don't let me see you lose your momentum.

- An object in motion tends to stay in motion—all I have to do is point you in the right direction.

- Your energy level generally seems appropriate for the tasks you need to accomplish here.

- Sometimes you seem a little lackadaisical or low-energy. Is everything okay?

Critical

- I'd like you to carry that early-morning energy throughout the day more consistently.

- I wish I could see just a little more energy and passion for the job coming from your cubicle.

- I am going to need you to pick up the pace—and the enthusiasm—just a little bit, please.

- The jury's still out on whether you have enough firepower to make it here.

- I can't have someone on staff who is unable to keep up with the rigorous pace. Can you?

- Your lack of energy and engagement are starting to concern me. What can we do to fix this?

- I feel like you're basically sleepwalking through your days. Are you getting enough rest?

Appraise an Employee's Self-Discipline

Glowing

- You are the kind of employee managers dream about: a highly disciplined self-starter.

- I've never had an employee who was so disciplined about her work.

- Your strong sense of discipline and tenacity are what make you such a valuable employee.

- You build self-discipline the way you build muscles: one day at a time.

- Without self-discipline, there is chaos; just remember that.

- All the talent in the world won't help you if you don't have the discipline to follow through.

Critical

- You have a lot of fire but no self-discipline to temper it with. I'd like to see you work on this.

- Your lack of self-discipline makes you fold like a paper tiger at the first sign of difficulty.

- Your lack of self-discipline is forcing others to pick up the slack. Are you okay with that?

- You will never attain any success in any field without the self-discipline to stick to things.

- I'd be extremely remiss in trusting an undisciplined person such as yourself with a job like this.

Appraise an Employee's Ability to Handle Stress

Praising

- It can be a pressure cooker here, but you always handle it with poise and aplomb.

- You seem impervious to the everyday stress we deal with here; what's your secret?

- I've never met someone who is so cool and collected under pressure; how do you do it?

- The way you handle yourself when the chips are down is admirable and to be commended.

- When others are wilting away in the heat, you just seem to thrive. What's your secret?

- You have incredible courage and calm under fire.

- In the crucible of stress that is this department, you just seem to emerge better for it.

- I admire the way you let stress slide off you like water off of a duck's back.

- You seem more like a seasoned veteran, the way you handle stress with such panache.

- You must be made of Teflon, the way stress and pressure just seem to bounce off of you.

- The fact that you excel under extreme pressure is one of the reasons we hired you.

- Stress is a fact of life; it's how we learn to handle it that counts.

- We all need to learn how to handle stress; it's a given in this industry.

- There's no way around stress and pressure; you just have to push through it as best you can.

- I understand it's tough to keep cool under pressure; how can we help you improve in this area?

- You seem to do pretty well under stress, but I'd like to see you do even better.

- I'm concerned that when the pressure ramps up, you just seem to run and hide.

- In order to succeed in this job you'll have to figure out a way to deal with the stress.

- As soon as an iceberg shows up, you are ready to abandon ship. You need to work on this.

- You fold like a house of cards whenever the stress level rises. I can't have that.

- Other people seem to be able to manage the stress here, but not you.

- It's unfair to the rest of the team that they have to carry your weight when you're stressed.

- Perhaps some biofeedback counseling or medication would help you.

- You're a liability because of your inability to roll with the punches.

Critical

Appraise an Employee's Ability to Handle Change

- Even when faced with rapid change, you always remain flexible and "steady as she goes."

- Your flexibility and willingness to embrace change are real assets to this company.

- You are the safe and secure harbor when the sea change is rapid and unpredictable.

- Your positive response to change is what makes you such a solid employee.

- The only thing that never changes is change. You seem to understand that pretty well.

- The only constant in life is change; we all need to learn to deal with it.

- Nobody can predict how someone will handle change, but I thought you'd do better.

- If I was thrown off at the first sign of change, how would I ever get anything done?

- To say I was disappointed in your reaction to these changes doesn't really cover it.

- Yes, change is scary, but it's only by embracing it that you can stay current.

- Adaptability and flexibility are necessary characteristics in any job; I suggest you learn more about this.

- The last thing we need here is another loose cannon who can't handle change.

- If you want to work in a place where things don't change, I suggest Never-Never Land.

Appraise an Employee's Ability to Handle Negative Feedback

- The thing I like about you is that you're not afraid to hear the truth about anything.

- Your openness to feedback, even when it's negative, is very unusual and refreshing.

- You show great maturity in the way you take feedback to heart and use it to your advantage.

- It's commendable that you view critiques and negative feedback as an opportunity to make things better.

- I think you handle negative feedback with grace and aplomb—a rare commodity these days.

- Anyone who can handle criticism as well as you, will always come out ahead.

- It's takes a very secure person to handle negative critiques with such equanimity.

- I'm glad that you are able to see my negative feedback for what it is: an investment in your future.

- Negative feedback isn't easy to hear, but generally speaking, I think you take it pretty well.

- I had a hard time with critiques at first, too, but I'm confident you'll get used to it.

- I know it hurts, but you need to realize that this is valuable information for you to have.

- Everyone gets negative feedback at some point; did you think you would be any different?

- Nobody likes to get bad news in a report, but you really need to learn to move past it.

- The fact that you get so upset at this feedback tells me you really don't want to hear it.

- How can you expect to improve if you don't look at your performance realistically and truthfully?

- You really need to be less emotionally invested in your job—and your ego.

- There is some give-and-take regarding feedback: I give it to you, and I expect you to take it.

- I think you need to buck up and just make the changes I've suggested.

- You can't possibly believe that you are without fault, now, can you?

- I think you need to calm down and then seriously consider the feedback you've been given.

- If I knew that you'd pop off at the first hint of negative feedback, I wouldn't have hired you.

- If you can't accept criticism, how will you ever grow or learn anything new?

- The fact that you can't take negative feedback makes you an unqualified employee.

- Whatever happened to the old adage: "What doesn't kill you makes you stronger"?

Critical

Appraise an Employee's Ability to Balance Work/Life Issues

Praising

- You always seem to handle the inevitable tug-of-war between work and life with equanimity.

- You seem to have an uncanny ability to strike just the right balance between work and life.

- I wish we could all maintain the balance you've struck between work and life issues.

- How do you juggle life and work issues so successfully? What's your secret?

- I really appreciate the fact that you keep your home life from impinging on work.

- I like that when you come here, you are all about work and nothing else.

- I can see that you are trying hard to keep personal issues from affecting your work.

- Believe me, I know how easy it is to let life get out of balance; maybe you need to work on this.

- Sometimes it seems as though the boundary between work and life is a bit blurred for you.

- A life out of balance is not a life that's worth living, in my opinion.

- We all have life issues. Most of us simply don't allow them to take center stage.

- A family is something you decided to take on, but your work still needs to take precedence.

- When work and family mix, it's usually not very pretty.

Critical

- I've noticed that you're having difficulties keeping work and life separated; what can we do about that?

- It's your responsibility to ensure that personal situations don't impinge on your job.

- Work is obviously your life, but I really need more well-balanced and versatile employees.

Appraise an Employee's Ability to See the Big Picture

Glowing

- When I need to pull back and see the larger issues, I know I can count on you to provide that.

- I love that you are always able to maintain a sense of the bigger picture in every situation.

- Most people can only see details, but you always seem able to see the larger context.

- I believe that we would all get lost in the details if you weren't here to help us appreciate the macro-view of things.

- Sometimes you lose sight of the big picture, but that happens to almost everyone.

- Yes, God is in the details, but success on this job can be found in the big picture.

- I know I can always count on you to point out the larger ramifications of any issue.

- You seem to get bogged down in extraneous details far too often. How can we fix this?

- You seem like more of a detail person. Would you agree?

Critical

- I think you are missing the forest for the trees most of the time.

- When you focus on the details, you lose sight of what's really important.

- Microscopes have their place, but you need to think more in terms of a telescope.

- You waste far too much time getting caught up in the details.

- It's a mystery how you got this far in the company with such a limited appreciation for the big picture.

Appraise an Employee's Ability to Deal With Adversity

Praising

- You have an uncanny ability to make the best of even the most adverse situation.

- When the going gets tough here, I know I can always call on you to help get us through.

- I'm always amazed at how you come out of every scrape unscathed.

- The phrase, "That which does not kill me makes me stronger," originally referred to you.

- There are very few employees who have the ability to survive—no, thrive—under adversity. You are one of them.

- I know I can always count on you to be the sturdy ship in troubled waters.

- Sometimes you seem a bit unnerved when adversity hits, but that happens to the best of us.

Critical

- Adversity is a fact of life—and work. I suggest you get used to it.

- When the going gets tough, the tough need to buck up and get going.

- I need to know that I can count on you when things get tough. Can I?

- The way you've been reacting to adversity lately concerns me. Can we talk about it?

- When you run from your troubles, you only end up creating more of them.

- Facing adversity presents a much less vulnerable part of you than running from it does.

- A big part of this job is learning to deal with adversity. Can you do this or not?

- At the merest whiff of trouble, you fold like a cheap suit in the rain.

- Perhaps I need to look for someone who doesn't abandon ship at the first sight of an iceberg.

Appraise an Employee's Sense of Responsibility

Approving

- The way you take responsibility for yourself and your work is to be commended.

- If everyone had the same sense of responsibility as you, we'd be in great shape.

- I know I can always trust you to take full responsibility for everything you do here.

- Don't shrink from taking responsibility for your work. Stand up and be accountable!

Critical

- I need to know that I can trust my people to be responsible. Can I trust you?

- Constantly abdicating your responsibility will not make you any friends here.

- A big part of being an adult involves standing up and taking responsibility for one's actions.

- Blame-shifting is for cowards and amateurs. I expected better from you.

- This is a team where blamers lose and the responsible get ahead and win.

- With power comes responsibility, but unfortunately you have neither–yet.

- You're about as responsible as a teenager at the mall with Daddy's credit card.

When an Employee Plays Devil's Advocate

Approving

- You are the one person here who saves us from groupthink. Thank you!

- Your unofficial function as devil's advocate in this department is essential to our success.

- I don't know what we would do without you to point out the potential negative consequences.

- Your willingness to entertain unpopular viewpoints is why we are so successful.

- Being able to bat all the issues around with you always seems to pay dividends later on.

- While it's a good idea to always consider other alternatives, your method is a bit alienating.

Critical

- It's good to know all the options, but we also need to be cognizant of all the time we're wasting.

- I'm grateful for your willingness to point out pitfalls, but your approach needs some tweaking.

- I appreciate your vigorous mind and love of debate, but it wastes too much time.

- I don't know if you realize it, but you are alienating the rest of the staff with your exhaustive–and exhausting–arguments.

- Your stance as devil's advocate is just making people feel demoralized. It has to stop!

- Yes, there are multiple sides to every argument–until you know the answer, and then there's just one.

When an Employee Oversteps the Company Hierarchy

Empathetic

- I know you are only trying to be helpful, but please remember who makes the final decisions.

- While we always value drive and energy, it's important not to step on any hierarchical toes.

- I like that you take on multiple projects, but just be cognizant of everyone's respective duties.

- I admire your go-getter attitude, but please just remember who is responsible for what around here.

- I can see that you want to be indispensable, but people feel as though you're invading their space.

- I appreciate your wiliness to fill the gap, but sometimes you end up nosing in where you're not wanted.

- Remember that we all have complementary skills here. Nobody can, or should, be doing it all.

- I think it would be better if you confined your excellent work to just your area of responsibility.

- People are starting to grumble that you are trying to take away their jobs. This won't do.

- I think we need to go over the company hierarchy one more time so that there's no confusion.

- I'd much prefer you stick to cleaning up your side of the street. You have enough to worry about.

- It's important that we all observe our respective roles within this company.

- I can't have a loose cannon running around and trying to run things. Please focus on your own work.

- If you want to take over these other jobs, you should request an official transfer.

- You're overstepping your boundaries and upsetting people. It needs to stop.

- Nobody really wants you sticking your nose into their department's affairs.

Direct

When an Employee Asks for a Promotion

Deserved

- Of course I will enthusiastically recommend you for a promotion, as it is most deserved.

- I would never presume to hold back my most valued and productive employee!

- There is no one more deserving of a promotion than you.

- I was actually going to bring this up. I'm looking forward to seeing you shine in your new role.

- There are other candidates on the list, but none is as deserving of promotion as you.

- I'm going to go right down to HR and submit your paperwork.

- Of course you can have the promotion. I hope you don't mind jumping right in.

- My only regret is that I didn't do this for you sooner. Congratulations!

- Would you be willing to accept a title change without a raise? Because that's the best I can do.

- I'd like to promote you right now, but let's just see how the next couple of months go.

- I'd like to table this until I have a better idea of how you're doing. Is that okay?

- I wish I could, but it's just not happening this year with all the cutbacks.

- Most people get promoted when they've created value for the company. What have you done?

- While I'd love to promote you, I just don't think you're ready yet. Maybe next year?

Undeserved

- I can't just promote you for no reason at all. You've got to sell me on the idea.

- If I promoted you now, it would look as though I was rewarding poor performance.

- I can't think of anyone who is less deserving of a promotion, sorry.

- A promotion? There is no way that is going to happen.

Part 5
Ethics

Even though Bernard Madoff is safely ensconced in jail, business ethics will continue to be a hot topic in the news, and will likely remain top-of-mind for you as a manager. If someone in your company has violated a safety regulation, challenged a social more, or broken a law, it's usually pretty obvious. You'll need to keep clear and exhaustive written records of everything, in case anything is challenged legally. And keep your HR department and legal counsel in the loop regarding any potentially explosive issues. And as always, make sure your own behavior is above reproach. This is *not* the time for "do as I say, not as I do"!

How to Appraise an Employee's Ethics

Praising

- It is a great comfort knowing that I never have to worry about your moral or ethical compass.

- Your ethics and morals are above reproach—a rare commodity in this day and age.

- With your unimpeachable character, you are a credit to this organization.

- It is rare to come across someone with such a finely honed conscience and sense of what is right.

- Talent and skills may come and go, but ethics and morals are forever.

- It's never been more important to run an ethical business. What are your thoughts on that?

- Solid ethics are the backbone of any prosperous business. I really hope you know that.

- Ethical behavior can be taught, so let's talk about some of the things you'll need to learn.

- How can I delegate tasks to you if I have trouble trusting you?

- Because I don't trust you to do the right thing, I have a hard time envisioning keeping you on.

- It's important to be above reproach in your behavior and character, both on and off the job.

- I know you don't want to be one of the Bernie Madoffs of this world, right?

- I don't have time to keep you on the straight and narrow. I hope you understand that.

Critical

- You're either ethical or you're not. I truly hope that you're on the right side of that equation.

- Taking the path of least resistance, morally and ethically, will never work out in the end, for you or for the company.

- If you were any more unethical, your employee ID photo would actually be a mug shot.

- If I allowed you to continue working here, I would have to designate myself as an accomplice.

Appraise an Employee's Honesty

Praising

- I know I can always count on you to give me the unvarnished truth about everything.

- I appreciate that I never have to second-guess you or check up on what you're telling me.

- If you were any more honest, I'd have to call you Abe. [*joking*]

- I know I can always trust you to speak the truth because you always do—even when it's difficult or unpleasant.

- If more of my employees were as honest as you, I'd have a lot fewer worries on the job.

- Not everyone appreciates a truth-teller, but I do. Just keep it up.

- I don't ever have to worry about where you stand on any topic or situation.

- I know that regardless of the situation, you're always going to make an honest decision.

Critical

- The number-one trait I look for in employees is honesty. Do you think of yourself as an honest person?

- I know you're not always comfortable speaking the truth, but it's really important that you do so.

- Sometimes it seems as though you exaggcratc or embellish the truth just a bit.

- I get the feeling that you are not always being 100-percent honest with me, and that concerns me.

- Our policy requires complete honesty and integrity here. I hope you're following this policy.

- If you were being honest with me right now, you'd admit that you don't always tell the truth.

- Someone who lies as easily as you do, has simply given himself permission to do so.

- You play so fast and loose with the truth, sometimes I wonder if you even know where it is anymore.

Appraise an Employee's Loyalty

Praising

- I know that when the chips are down, you will be the last person standing with me and the company.

- We need more passionately loyal employees like you.

- Your loyalty is unimpeachable and to be commended.

- You've made the goals and values of our company your own. That's the very definition of loyalty.

- Yes, you seem to be committed to this company, but it doesn't seem all that genuine.

- We are loyal to our employees. The question is, will you be loyal to us?

- There is nothing worse than disloyalty among my ranks. Don't ever make that mistake.

- We consider this place like a family. You wouldn't throw your family under the bus, would you?

- Why should I trust you if you're disloyal when the chips are down?

- I'm not asking for heroic self-sacrifice—just ordinary loyalty that one would ask of even the lowliest servant.

- Most people are most loyal to the person who signs their paycheck, no?

- I'm actually hurt that you would even consider throwing us under the bus like that.

- Loyalty has nothing to do with performance, and everything to do with trust.

- I feel as though we have a traitor in our midst. Please tell me that isn't the case.

- If you don't have our backs, there's no reason we should have yours, either.

- I can't pay anyone to work here who isn't 100-percent onboard and committed.

- Perhaps you would be more comfortable working alone; that way, you wouldn't have to decide where your loyalty lies.

Critical

Appraise an Employee's Attendance

Approving

- No matter what happens, I can always count on you to be right here at your desk, doing your job.

- I've never seen you miss even a single day. How do you do it?

- If we gave awards for perfect attendance, you would certainly get one.

- You are one of the few people who is always here, come hell or high water.

- Sometimes I wish you *would* take some time off; you never seem to take a break! [*joking*]

- I know I can always count on you to make it in, even when the weather is bad.

- I feel confident knowing I can count on you to be here, even when I'm not.

- You do take a lot of time off, but as long as your work doesn't suffer, I don't care.

- Your attendance has been decent in general, although I do see that you tend to take Fridays off.

- I'm concerned that you've been missing so much work. Is anything wrong?

- Everyone else seems to make it in on a consistent basis. Why is this difficult for you?

- I would encourage you to make your attendance here more–shall we say–regular.

- If your attendance doesn't improve, I'm afraid we'll need to talk about the next steps.

- If I have to *tell* you to come in to work, perhaps we need to rethink your employment here.

Critical

- I can't be signing over a paycheck to a consistent no-show.

- You're here so infrequently, some people don't even know who you are.

- You either have some serious problems or you're the laziest employee I've ever had.

- As they say, 90 percent of the job is showing up, but you don't even do that.

Appraise an Employee's Attention to Safety

Praising

- I know I can always count on you to adhere to the letter of the law when it comes to safety.

- I appreciate the fact that you always put safety first, no matter what.

- Your attention to the rules of safety has made this a safer, better place to work.

- You seem a bit lax in the safety department; perhaps we should go over the manual again?

- It's better to be safe than sorry. Please let me see some serious improvement in this area.

- Most of the team is much more safety-oriented than you. You need to step it up.

- Sometimes I'm afraid that you're going to get in a bad accident. Please don't let that happen!

- You need to not only safeguard yourself, but also those around you. Please start taking this seriously.

- Right now, you are more of a liability than an asset. What can we do about that?

Critical

- Your idea of safety seems more like an after-thought than a real commitment to avoiding accidents.

- I can't have someone like you running around and putting everyone's lives in danger.

- When you spell "safety" it reads W-R-E-C-K-L-E-S-S.

- Forget the Occupational Safety and Health Administration. You're a threat to everyone who enters this building.

- You have a disregard for safety that borders on the pathological.

- Yes, you're productive, but you are also far too reckless and dangerous to keep on.

Appraise an Employee's Adherence to Policies and Procedures

Praising

- You always adhere to the letter of the law when it comes to the way we do business.

- I admire your attention to detail and investment in/adherence to our policies and procedures.

- I really love the fact that you never cut corners and always do things by the book.

- I know I can always trust you to do things the right way, the way *we* do them.

- Your consistent attention to our policies and procedures is laudable.

- *I'm* not that observant of our company handbook!

- While adherence to policy isn't the most important trait for success, I do appreciate your commitment.

- Most of our policies are self-explanatory, but maybe we should go over some of them.

- Sometimes I question how thorough your knowledge is of our policies and procedures.

- You seem to just ignore how we prefer to do things. Why is that?

- I'm not expecting slavish devotion to the rules, just a basic understanding of how we operate.

- *Knowing* our policies and procedures is only half the equation; you have to actually *follow* them.

- It seems like you just give lip service to our rules and regulations. This needs to change.

- Someone who refuses to follow our policies is just too much of a liability, I'm afraid.

- Because you will only play by your own rules, you will never make it in this culture.

- We write our policies down for a reason, not to pass time or see our words in print.

- I am not interested in having a loose cannon in the department. Either straighten up and fly right or you're through.

Critical

When an Employee Is Caught Lying

Lax

- There is no way I can point a bony finger at you; after all, I lie to you guys all the time! [*joking*]

- Everyone lies; the main thing is not to get caught. [*joking*]

- Look, we all lie, but the ones who get away with it are just a bit more subtle about it.

- Please just don't let any of your lies come back to bite me or the department.

- Maybe we misunderstood what you said. Would you care to rephrase that?

- I'm sure you meant no harm, but please know that this sort of thing is not acceptable here.

- Now that your lies have been uncovered, let's see how we can salvage this situation.

- You've been a great employee otherwise, so I want to give you a second chance.

- I'd hate to see you ruin your chance for success here with one more lie. Don't let it happen.

- Tell me what *you* think would be an appropriate response to catching someone in a lie.

- We all tell white lies from time to time, but a major lie like this can't go unpunished.

- Spreading disinformation will only result in your getting fired at some point.

- I have no use for someone on my team who plays so fast and loose with the truth.

- No one on my watch is going to get away with lying on the job.

Punitive

- People lie to protect themselves, to get something, or to avoid something. So which one is it?

- You lie so glibly that I wonder if you aren't a sociopath or something.

- How do I know you're lying? Your mouth is moving. [*sarcasm*]

When an Employee Steals Intellectual Property

Lax

- You just let your slip show. We all do it from time to time.

- It's virtually impossible to know about all this stuff and not let anything slip out.

- Look, ideas are out there for *anyone* to take; just don't get caught next time.

- I'm sure you didn't mean any harm. Maybe next time try to draw on your own good ideas?

- Everyone appropriates the ideas of others. Just look at Steve Jobs.

- I know you have plenty of good ideas of your own. I wouldn't have hired you otherwise.

- Stealing ideas shows a lack of self-confidence; how can I encourage you so it doesn't happen again?

- This may seem like a small thing, but it wasn't to the person you stole from.

- This just makes you look small and petty—and incompetent. Is that what you want?

- Have you always done this kind of thing to get ahead?

Punitive

- If it happens again, I will make sure that every potential employer finds out about this.

- Stealing intellectual property is not only unethical and dirty; it's criminal.

- You've violated our honor code as well as everyone's trust, and for that I have to fire you.

- I hope the money you received will be consolation as you stand on the unemployment line.

When an Employee Sexually Harasses a Colleague

Lax

- Look, I get that he/she is attractive. Just try and tone it down a bit, okay?

- I'm not saying you have to act like a nun/monk. Just try and be more discrete.

- Look, I didn't write the rules; I just enforce them. It's probably better to knock it off.

- This company has an official policy about sexual harassment. Did you know that?

- When you harass someone on the job, you've crossed a line that needs to be addressed.

- If I were to look the other way I would be just as culpable, if not more so.

- Your behavior is unprofessional and hurtful. Either it stops now or you're through.

- Do you really expect me to look the other way when you're violating company policy?

- I cannot allow you to continue to sexually harass your colleagues.

Punitive

- If you don't have control over your behavior, I'll have to step in and control it for you.

- There is no excuse for this kind of disgusting behavior. I'm going to have to write you up.

- You are so far over the line that you don't even know where the line is anymore.

- Please try to convince me you're not the creeper/ stalker that I think you are.

- The kind of behavior you display is like a cancer. Unfortunately, I'm going to need to officially excise you.

When an Employee Bullies Others

Lax

- I appreciate your strong, domineering personality; just try to take a more empathic stance next time.

- I know it's hard not to let your emotions run things, but you need to tone it down a bit.

- They may have deserved whatever you dished out, but there are still rules of behavior we need to observe.

- Your colleagues sometimes feel nervous in your presence. Does that concern you at all?

- People often bully others when they feel disenfranchised or insecure. How can I best support you so it doesn't continue?

- It is easier to change your behavior than it is to change your beliefs.

- I'm sure you have very good reasons for acting this way, but it still needs to stop.

- Do you feel comfortable controlling people with fear? Do you really think they respect you?

- Wouldn't you rather motivate others with the carrot rather than the stick?

- I think deep down you act this way because you are afraid. What do you think?

- You can't go on railroading other people all day. Please, learn how to play well with others.

- You may think that you're accomplishing something by acting this way, but you're not.

- This is a no-bullying zone, just so you know.

- You know what happens to bullies in the movies: They always get their comeuppance.

- This is an environment of caring and support, and your behavior is flying in the fact of that.

- All the good you do here is negated by your egregious—and unnecessary—bullying behavior.

- You're a fox in the henhouse and a liability to me. Either you get your act together or you're through.

- We have rules and regulations about this kind of thing. I suggest you familiarize yourself with them.

- Tell me why I should keep you on after you've essentially ruined the morale in this department.

- Now that you've shown us who you really are, let me show you who *we* really are: You're fired.

Punitive

When an Employee Fakes Injury or Illness

Subtle

- I'm sure you have a very good reason for missing so much work.

- I'm really not used to my employees taking so many sick days. Should I be concerned?

- You do seem to take an awful lot of time off. Is anything wrong that we should know about?

- Admittedly I am concerned with the amount of days you're missing. Is there anything I should know?

- Your health is more important than anything, of course. It's just that I have a business to run.

- I feel terrible that you're sick so often. So what did the doctor say about all of this?

- You sure seem to be a magnet for injuries and illnesses. Have you always been this way?

- It's not that I don't believe you; we just need a doctor's note for our records.

- I feel badly that you're suffering. Fortunately, we all have the ability to work from home.

- It's standard procedure here that we document all major illnesses and injuries.

- You seem to always be sick on Fridays and Mondays. I wonder why that might be.

- We're geared toward helping all employees with their health issues, but this seems a little extreme.

- Sometimes I get the feeling you're not being 100-percent honest. It's probably just my imagination.

- Personally I think you're just "trolling" with all these sick days. I'll be watching you.

Blunt

When an Employee Uses the Internet Improperly

Lax

- If everyone else is doing it, well–what can I say?

- As long as all the work gets done, I really don't care what you do in your spare time.

- Look, we all surf the Web from time to time. Just tone it down a little, okay?

- Internet abuse is pretty common these days. How do you feel you are doing in that regard?

- Using the Internet here is a privilege, not a right. It can be revoked at any time.

- I'd like to think that we are all adult enough to use the Internet properly and with self-control.

- I've noticed that you've been surfing the Internet during work hours. This needs to stop.

- The Internet is a tool. Please use it only to accomplish company goals.

- You do know that we have a policy regarding use of the Internet, don't you?

- If you can't get this under control I'm going to have to crack down on the entire department.

- If you're addicted to Web surfing you need to get some kind of help.

Punitive

When an Employee Makes Excessive Personal Calls

Lax

- I don't mind personal calls at all. Just make sure you're not flaunting it in front of management.

- I don't care how much you yak on the phone; just don't let it affect your productivity.

- Look, we all need to make phone calls now and then. Just be more discrete about it.

- Emergency calls are okay. I just don't like to see you spending time chatting when you could be working.

- Think of it as being on a continuum: there is reasonable phone use, and then there is *your* habit. Your ability to make personal calls is a privilege, not a right. Don't make me revoke it.

- Just think of all of the hours you've spent on the phone, when you could've been working.

- Now I can see why your productivity has taken such a nosedive: you've been spending all your time chatting on the phone.

- If you can't curb your phone use during business hours, I'm going to have to write you up.

- You do realize that by chatting on the phone like this, you're literally stealing from the company.

- I'm not going to pay you to basically chat on the phone all day. You need to knock it off!

- By wasting valuable time on the phone, you're actually stealing money from the company.

- In the future I'll simply deduct the time you spend chatting from your paycheck. That ought to fix it.

Punitive

- Do you think that somehow the rules governing phone use don't apply to you? Think again.

- I could just confiscate your phone at the door, but we're not the Gestapo.

- If only I could get you to pay as much attention to your work as you do to your cell phone.

- We can put a man on the moon, but apparently there's nothing to stop you from using your phone during business hours.

When an Employee Is Using Alcohol or Drugs

Hands-Off

- My policy about this stuff is "don't ask, don't tell."

- The only thing I can speak to around here is your performance. The other stuff is not my affair.

- This really isn't my business but I admit that I am a bit concerned about your well-being.

- Look, I don't care if you have a three-martini lunch; just try to keep it under control.

- This is probably just a phase you're going through, right?

- I can see that you aren't yourself lately. I am here if you need to talk to anyone.

- I know that you've been self-medicating. I'm not judging you; I am just concerned.

- We are all very worried about you and want you to get help. Will you do that?

- I really don't care what you do on your personal time, but you can't come to work like this.

- You're not only hurting yourself; you're hurting others who have to take up your slack.

- I don't want to punish you, but I do think you need to understand how serious this is.

- We have company regulations against using alcohol and drugs on the job. Please review them.

- How can you expect to be able to get your work done when you're walking around in a fog?

- This is not only against company regulations, it is also illegal.

- I will never allow this kind of behavior on my watch. Please go home and sober up.

- We have very strict rules about using drugs or alcohol on the job and we expect you to comply.

- Unfortunately, I'm going to have to get the CEO and your family involved. This has gone too far.

- I simply cannot condone the use of drugs or alcohol on these premises.

- If you want to succeed here, you'd better keep yourself clean and sober from now on.

Involved

When an Employee Steals

Lax

- They call it "petty" theft for a reason. It's petty and silly to make a big deal about it.

- Everyone steals at least once in their life. Just please make sure this happens only once.

- Look, I'm not lily-white either, but you really need to be more careful how you conduct yourself.

- I'm sure it was all a misunderstanding. It's probably best to return what you took, however.

- I'm really interested in hearing the reasons why you did this. Strictly *entre nous*, don't worry.

- I don't want to punish you or anything; just tell me what's going on.

- It's more that I'm personally hurt than anything else. Why did you do it?

- I'm not looking to prosecute anyone. I just want to understand why you felt the need to do this.

- I'll look the other way this one time, but next time I'll have to write you up.

- You're an otherwise stellar employee; I really don't understand why you felt the need to steal.

- I know times are tough right now, which is why I am going to give you a pass on this.

- I know that you're guilty, but I won't mention anything to anyone unless it happens again.

- Now that you've violated our trust in this manner, you'll be hard-pressed to win it back now, if ever.

- Unfortunately, this must be written into your evaluation. I'm not sure what the next steps will be.

Punitive

- This kind of thing is not only against rules and regulations; it's also illegal.

- This isn't a court of law; you need to prove to me that you *didn't* do it.

- Stealing is one of the worst things anyone can do to their employer.

- I never thought of you as the kind of person who would do something like this.

- If I didn't punish you, I would be setting a pretty poor example for the rest of team.

- Consider this your final warning: if it happens again, you'll be without a job.

- I'm not interested in keeping criminals on my staff. You're through here.

When an Employee Is Disruptive

Lax

- I know you don't mean any harm, but perhaps it would be better to tone it down a bit.

- I want all of my employees to be able to express themselves; just try and keep it reasonable.

- I appreciate your energy and passion, but sometimes it's a bit over-the-top.

- I want to know what you're thinking, but maybe you could couch things a bit more gently.

- Of course I always want to hear your opinion. But there is way to do it so that it's not disruptive.

- Please just pause and think the next time you feel the need to act out in this manner.

- It's not necessary to be loud and disruptive to get your point across. Just talk to me.

- There is a time and a place for everything—except this kind of disruptive behavior.

- The other employees are growing frustrated with your acting out. How do you feel about that?

- We have guidelines for how employees should voice their concerns or objections. Please follow them.

- I can't have such a loose cannon on my staff. Let's figure out how we can fix this before it's too late.

- We have standards and rules around here and we expect everyone to abide by them.

- When you disrupt the team in this manner, you are really just hurting yourself in the process.

- Have you ever listened to yourself when you go off like this? It's really quite astonishing.

- People can't work when you're raising the roof about every little thing. Knock it off!

- This is the last time I'll warn you about this. If it happens again, you'll be written up.

- I've worked hard to create a serene and supportive environment here, and I expect you to honor that.

- I'm not interested in having Shrek on my team. Either be respectful or you're out.

- You're going to just have to recognize that you're not the only one in the office.

- You've now managed to alienate everyone who works here, including me.

Punitive

When an Employee Leaks Company Information

Lax

- I am sure you meant no harm, but next time please think before you speak.

- I know your intentions were good. Just play your cards a bit more closely to your chest.

- I know you didn't mean any harm; next time I'm sure you'll think twice before blabbing.

- Next time just ask yourself whether it's necessary, advisable, or even helpful to share information.

- Your access to this information is a privilege. Please don't make me take that away from you.

- Employees who give away sensitive information to competitors usually don't last here.

- The fact that you've put this information out there puts us all at risk.

- We have regulations regarding proprietary information. You must adhere to them.

- I don't want to get you in hot water, so for now I'll just be giving you a verbal warning.

- I'm just curious as to why you thought it would be a good idea to share this information.

- Do you not know what the word *confidential* means? Perhaps you should look it up.

- You are playing with the big boys now. Are you sure you're up to it?

- You're just a mediocre, mid-level employee who fancies himself an industrial spy.

Punitive

- Now we have to scramble to plug up all the leaks you've spring.

- Perhaps you should pause and reflect on the consequences the next time you feel the urge to blab.

- Have you never heard the phrase: "Loose lips sink ships"?

- I'm not sure what your motivation was, but you must know that you've put us at a huge disadvantage.

- I can't have a defector spy working on my team. I'm going to have to let you go.

When an Employee Is Absent Often

Lax

- You do seem to take a lot of days, but as long as the work gets done, it's okay.

- I don't care if you're here or not, as long as everything gets done on time.

- You're out so often, I've forgotten that you even work here! [*joking*]

- I'm sure you have a very good reason for missing work. How's your productivity?

- I am worried that you are out so often. Is everything okay?

- There is no shame in failure. However, there is shame in not even showing up to fail.

- I hope you know just how important good attendance is. Please show me that you do.

- I would really like to see your smiling face at your desk much more often.

- You do know that just showing up is 90 percent of the battle, don't you?

- The employees who show up are the ones who get ahead. I hope you understand that.

- Your team has had to work overtime to pick up your slack. Are you really okay with that?

- From now on I'll be watching you carefully. Please don't ignore this warning.

- I'd love to know how you justify missing so much work. Please, enlighten me. [*sarcasm*]

- It should not be a shock to management when you actually show up. Wouldn't you agree?

- Is that you're just not happy here? Because we can certainly arrange a remedy for that.

- Believe me, I notice who is here and who isn't. You're not going to get away with this.

- I so rarely get a chance to meet a man of leisure. However do you do it? [*sarcasm*]

Punitive

Part 6

Communication

In far too many companies, communication breakdowns are the cause of hurt feelings, wasted time, and missed deadlines. This is completely ironic, given how many wonderful avenues of communication we have at our disposal: email, text message, Skype, fax—you name it! How did this happen, and what's the remedy?

You can't expect your employees to be great communicators if they never hear from you or you're not good at it. So, set the tone in your office and raise the bar for all concerned. Each and every email, letter, memorandum, and instant message represents an opportunity to either clarify or obfuscate, to expedite or delay, to ameliorate a situation or make it much worse. Show your employees what an effective and professionally crafted email looks like, and how a clear and concise memo should read. Be consistent and *walk the walk* yourself.

How's that for clear communication?

Appraise an Employee's Listening Skills

Approving

- You are such a careful and attentive listener, I don't think you miss a thing that anyone says.

- Everyone here seems to go to you as a sounding board for advice.

- You understand that being a good communicator involves listening closely and thoughtfully.

- You are the kind of person to whom others turn when they need someone to talk to.

- You are one of the few people I know who listens more often than they speak.

- Not only do you listen thoughtfully and attentively, but you retain everything that is said.

- While you are a good communicator, sometimes I think you could be better at the listening part.

- I know you always have something important to say, but sometimes it's better just to listen.

- The ability to listen thoughtfully is something I really value in my employees.

- Sometimes it seems as though you aren't listening, but just waiting for the other person to finish speaking.

- There is a reason we have two ears and only one mouth. Think about it.

- If people don't feel heard by you, they are going to stop talking. Is that what you want?

- I'd like to see you make active listening more of a habit, starting today.

- No one wants to work with you anymore. You simply run roughshod over everyone.

Critical

Appraise an Employee's Verbal Communication

Praising

- Communicating with you is always a pleasure. You make everyone's job easier.

- I appreciate that you always keep those lines of communication open with everyone.

- I love that you always speak with clarity, conviction, and, above all, respectfulness.

- You always speak your mind, but you still manage not to alienate anyone in the process.

- You not only have great ideas, but you communicate them well, too.

- In general, I think you do a good job of getting your points across.

- You're not the most eloquent person, but you are good at making yourself heard.

- Sometimes it's not always clear what you are getting at. Perhaps this is something you could work on.

- I'd like to see you work a little harder at your communication skills.

- If we can't all communicate with clarity and respect, we'll never get anything done.

- Everything you say only serves to confuse and obfuscate. Is that what you want?

- What good is all that talent, skill, and experience if you can't get anything across to others?

- If I communicated the way you did, you would have no idea what I was talking about.

- Your defensive communication style gets in the way of finding advantageous solutions.

- I don't think you could communicate your way out of a paper bag.

Critical

Appraise an Employee's Written Communication

Praising

- No one in this department is your equal when it comes to written communications.

- Your written communications are always excellent: clear, cogent, and concise.

- Your writing skills are beyond reproach.

- You are such a good writer that I rarely have to edit anything you submit.

- Everyone always appreciates your clear and professional communiqués.

- I like that you adjust your writing style according to its purpose and audience.

- In general I have no issues with the way you express yourself on paper or electronically.

- Sometimes I wish you would put a little more thought and care into your written communiqués.

- You could be a very passable writer if you just made more of an effort.

- Everything you write is a reflection on this company. Just remember that.

- Sometimes I think you just hit Send without proofreading your work.

- You have to understand that corporate communiqués are not text messages to your friends.

- I recommend that someone else review all your communiqués before they are sent out.

- Your writing is atrocious: sloppy, unprofessional, and careless. You need to take some classes.

Critical

- Other than your abysmal writing skills, I have no issue with your work here.

- From now I am going to have so-and-so write up all your documents. We can't afford any more errors.

Appraise an Employee's Body Language

Admiring

- I like that you always comport yourself with professionalism, friendliness, and ease.

- You always have such a confident yet open and friendly demeanor.

- You say more with just actions than others do in a book full of words.

- You are a person of integrity in that your body language always matches what you are saying.

- You need to be more cognizant of what your body language is saying when you are speaking.

- Sometimes you say a mouthful without ever uttering a word.

- I am amazed at how much you can express without even opening your mouth.

- Do you realize how closed off and unfriendly your posture and body language are?

- You are *saying* "Talk to me" but your body language says "Buzz off."

- You really need to take a look in a mirror at how you comport yourself.

- Nonverbal communication comprises 60 percent of your meaning. Did you realize that?

- When your words and body language don't match, you confuse the people you are talking to.

Critical

Appraise an Employee's Conflict-Resolution Skills

Praising

- With you here, I know that even the most heated conflict will get resolved with ease.

- You have a wonderful ability to resolve even the trickiest conflicts with skill and grace.

- You have a way of disarming angry people and diffusing tense situations.

- I am thankful to have a calm and skilled mediator like you on my team.

- When there is strife, I know I can count on you to diffuse things.

- Did you take conflict-resolution classes in college? Because you're very good at it.

- Sometimes you seem a bit out of your depth when things get heated. Maybe we can work on that.

- Conflicts don't get worse when you're around, but they don't get much better, either.

- I would like to see you get more comfortable handling and diffusing tension in the department.

- You have a lot of common sense when it comes to resolving conflict. You just need more tact.

- I would like you to see you diffusing conflict in the department, not adding to it.

- You can't run away or hide from conflict; it's everywhere, even here.

- There will always be conflict and adversity; it's how you handle it that counts.

Critical

- You seem to run and hide at the first sign of adversity. How can we fix this?

- Resolving conflict is a learned skill. I'd like you to learn more about it in the months ahead.

- Conflicts tend to spiral out of control unless people are able to act rationally. Can you?

- You seem completely out of your depth when things get heated. How can we fix that?

- You give up at the first sign of trouble. I can't afford such cowardly behavior on my team.

Appraise an Employee's Assertiveness

Praising

- Your assertiveness strikes just the right balance between friendliness and aggressiveness.

- You are just the kind of assertive person we need to take control and make our path clear.

- It is refreshing to be working with someone who has chutzpah in just the right measure.

- It's great that when we need someone to take charge, you simply say, "Bring it on!"

- I know you are able and willing to take the bull by the horns if and when it becomes necessary.

- Although it doesn't come naturally, I'm glad you're willing to take charge at critical junctures.

- I know that taking charge isn't everyone's forte, but you seem really uncomfortable with it.

- Your best ideas will come to naught if you don't have the assertiveness to broadcast them.

Critical

- I don't know what we'll do if we don't get some take-charge people around here.

- I just wish you would take some risks and be more willing to speak up sometimes.

- I'm concerned that your otherwise sound work will get lost because of your timidity.

- If you're unwilling or unable to assert yourself, you won't go very far in any industry.

- When I hired you I didn't think that I was hiring a shrinking violet.

Appraise an Employee's E-mails

Praising

- You always put in extra effort to make all of your e-mails clear, concise, and cohesive.

- You always treat e-mails as the professional corporate communications that they are.

- I wish the rest of team took as much care with their e-mails as you do.

- In general, I have no complaints with your e-mails to colleagues or clients.

- I'd like you to invest a bit more time and care when you compose your e-mails.

- It's easy to fall into the habit of being too casual in one's e-mails, but that needs to stop.

- I know you mean well, but there is really no place for shorthand in your e-mails to clients.

- Maybe we can brainstorm ways to keep your e-mails friendly without resorting to silly emoticons.

Critical

- You seem a bit out of your depth when it comes to composing appropriate, well-written e-mails. Let's review.

- E-mails should be saved and then re-read before you send them. Otherwise you may risk offending someone.

- As far as company e-mails go, I've certainly seen worse.

- You need to proofread your messages before you send them; otherwise, you're reflecting poorly on the company.

- E-mail is not the place for you to dump all your emotions and frustrations. Just stick to the facts.

- Your e-mails leave a wake of confused and angry customers in their wake. Why is that?

- Have you never heard of the Undo feature?

Appraise an Employee's Letter-Writing Skills

Praising

- No matter what the medium, you always express yourself with clarity and conviction.

- You have a way of phrasing things perfectly when you write your letters. What's your secret?

- Whenever I need a well-crafted written document, I know I can always turn to you.

- Writing seems to come effortlessly to you—is this a natural ability or did you learn it?

- You write beautifully, with clarity, concision, and cohesiveness.

- Your letter writing-skills are a real boon to this company. We are grateful to have you!

- You have an ability to tailor your writing to the specific context each and every time.

- Your letters to clients are about average: no worse or better than those of most people.

- Your letters aren't deathless prose, but they get the job done.

- No one will fault you for writing a letter that isn't perfect every now and then.

- Your writing is, in general, pretty good, but I think you could invest a bit more effort in it.

- I'd like to see you really start raising the bar with your written communiqués.

- Sometimes I question the quality of your writing. Perhaps a quick brush-up is in order?

- I wish you were a better writer, but we can't afford to hire anyone new right now.

- I know you are doing your best, but that is what concerns me.

- I'd like to review your letters before they get sent out. Are you okay with that?

- I am keeping an eye on your "wordsmithing." I can't afford to have you offend any more customers.

- I know we're not paying you as a writer, but how can you even call this letter "writing"?

Critical

Appraise an Employee's Phone Skills

Approving

- I am so relieved to have someone as capable as you as our first line of defense on the phone.

- Your phone manner is exactly what it should be: professional, friendly, and helpful.

- Sometimes I think you're better on the phone than you are in person! [*joking*]

- I love that you can basically field any kind of call in your sleep. What a valuable skill!

- Your skill at handling people on the phone is impressive.

- Using the phone is almost a lost art, but you certainly seem to have a handle on it.

- Handling the phones isn't everyone's forte, but you seem fairly capable.

- I know you are trying, but you need to bump up your phone skills just a notch.

- I've definitely heard people who are much less skilled on the phone than you.

- Just because you're on the phone doesn't mean that you shouldn't be completely professional.

- You and the phone really don't seem to get along. Why is that?

- Maybe you would feel more comfortable in a position that doesn't require you to speak on the phone.

- All it takes to succeed on the phone is opposable thumbs and a willingness to help.

Critical

- I can't have you acting like that the phone, insulting people, muddling issues, and losing your cool.

- Please do something to get rid of the disinterested monotone; you're alienating customers.

- If I don't see a real improvement in your phone manner, we'll need to make other arrangements.

Part 7

Productivity

Here is where the rubber meets the road: are your employees getting everything done properly and on time? Much of this depends on how clearly you've communicated expectations. Assuming you've already done this, how can you best assess the productivity of your employees?

Some companies do it by using simple metrics: *Who sold the most widgets? Who fixed the most bugs? Who processed the most cases?* Sometimes it's easy to tell when an employee is slipping behind—she'll miss deadlines, her work quality will suffer, or she'll be absent more and more often. Whatever the case, this section will enable you to communicate your expectations and feedback clearly and concisely. It will also help keep productivity running at optimum speed and efficiency.

Appraise an Employee's Productivity

Appreciative

- You not only meet, but exceed our expectations with regard to productivity.

- You get the most done of anyone here, but you make it look easy.

- You are by far the most productive employee I've ever had on staff.

- You do the work of at least five people, easily. How do you do it?

- You're so productive, sometimes I feel as though I am overloading you with work.

- As far as productivity goes, you get by, but I'd like to see you raise the bar next quarter.

- I know you've struggled with staying productive. I appreciate how much you've been trying.

- We all need to be able to take our own inventory— how do you think your productivity has been?

- Do *you* feel that you are as productive as you ought to be? Why or why not?

- I know you are doing your best in terms of productivity, but it really needs to be better.

- You've had your productive moments; I'd just like to see more of them.

- I know you have it in you to be the most productive employee here. Prove me right!

- The numbers don't lie: you are not living up to your productivity objectives.

Critical

- What is it that you do here, anyway? Because you have virtually nothing to show for your time.

- How is it possible for you to be so unproductive? Are you perhaps asleep on the job?

- I don't see why I should continue to cut a check to someone who clearly doesn't produce.

Appraise an Employee's Work Quality

Praising

- I have nothing but praise and kudos to offer you in terms of the quality of your work.

- For you, quality is always job one.

- In terms of overall work quality, you raise the bar around here and inspire others to do likewise.

- Your work is always of unimpeachable quality. Well done!

- You always do your utmost, and it shows in the very high-quality work you do.

- You are only satisfied in giving everything your best, and it shows.

- Some people are satisfied with achieving less than their best; are you one of them?

- You get a lot done, but I don't know that it's the highest quality you're capable of.

- The cream always rises to the top. Show me what you're *really* capable of.

- Anything worth doing is worth doing well; wouldn't you agree?

Critical

- I will only accept the highest-quality work from my employees, and that includes you.

- You make me and the company look bad when you give anything less than your best.

- You can't breeze your way through each day and expect to win any accolades for quality.

- You don't know the meaning of the word quality. You don't even know how to spell it.

Appraise an Employee's Ability to Set and Achieve Goals

Praising

- Whenever you set a goal, I know that you are certain to achieve it.

- I admire how you create a plan and then stick to it until it's completed.

- Anyone can set goals, but it takes a person of tenacity to make them come to fruition.

- Your ability to set and achieve goals, both short- and long-term, is to be commended.

- Let's go over some of your goals together; that way I can track your progress until you get the hang of it.

- You always start well, but you have a hard time seeing things through to completion.

- You seem to have difficulty setting and achieving goals. What can I do to help you with that?

- For you, goals are like New Year's Eve resolutions: easy to make, not so easy to keep.

- If you fail to plan, you may as well plan to fail.

Critical

- He who aims at nothing hits it every time. Is that what you want?

- Hope is not a plan, you know.

- You seem pretty apathetic when it comes to setting goals. That needs to change.

- Follow-through is what I want from you, but it is up to you to make it happen.

- We're not paying you to coast aimlessly through your days. You need to learn how to set goals and realize them.

Appraise an Employee's Reliability

Praising

- We like to call you "Old Faithful" because we know we can always depend on you.

- With such a reliable person on staff, I feel secure knowing that everything will get done.

- When we want something done, we know we can always count on you to make it happen.

- You are by far the most dependable, reliable person I've ever had on staff.

- Talent is nothing without reliability, and you have both, in spades.

- Everyone drops the ball sometimes. Just try not to make a habit of it.

- None of us is perfect, but in your case I think you need to tighten up the slack a little.

- I, too, struggled with letting people down at one time. Let's work on this together.

- Fortunately, reliability is something that can be learned. I know it's hard, but it's a necessity.

- I know you mean well, but sometimes you seem flighty and unreliable. Can you work on that?

- Your lack of dependability undermines the good work that you do. Don't let that happen.

- You're a good person, but I just can't count on you. Please work on this before your next review.

- Do you really want to be the last person to be picked for the team because we can't count on you?

- If I can't count on you to do what you say you're doing to do, how can I keep you on?

- I know you don't mean to, but your unreliability is really starting to tick people off.

- You need to grow up and learn that you are as only as relied upon as you are reliable.

- You wouldn't draw the ire of your colleagues if you just followed through on tasks.

- I want to help you become more dependable, but I can't go around holding your hand.

- You're smart and you work hard, but we just can't depend on you when the chips are down.

- When you fail to follow through, you end up hurting everyone, not just yourself.

- I know I can always count on you: you *always* let me down.

Critical

Appraise the Consistency of an Employee's Work

Admiring

- You consistently produce work of the very highest quality.

- I know I can always count on your work to be consistently excellent.

- Your work is not only consistent, but it is also of the very highest quality.

- Your work is the most consistent I've ever seen.

- I have never seen anyone deliver finished work of such consistent quality.

- You can write your own ticket in the industry if your work remains as constantly great as this.

- I only wish I could have been as consistent when I was your age.

- Your work is always on time, under budget, and consistently of the highest quality.

- You are the most consistent producer I've ever had the privilege of having on my staff.

- I can always count on your work being the best of all the staffers.

- Without fail, your work is of a very consistent quality.

- It's rare that you don't keep up that consistent standard of excellence in your work.

- Most of the time your work is good. I'd just like that to be the case all of the time.

- You show flashes of brilliance with your work, but your overall record is spotty at best.

Critical

- *Everyone* has their ups and downs in the consistency of their work from time to time.

- I'd really like to see more consistency in your productivity and overall work quality.

- Your work is so uneven that I am not sure you'd really want me to evaluate it.

- We have a failure to communicate regarding consistency; I want it, but you can't seem to deliver it.

- The only consistent thing about your work is its inconsistency.

- Yes your work is consistent: it's consistently *bad*.

Appraise an Employee's Ability to Meet Deadlines

Praising

- I know I can always count on your to meet or exceed every deadline, no matter how unrealistic.

- Without fail, you are always on time or early with every project. How do you do it?

- I appreciate the alacrity and punctuality with which you meet every deadline.

- In general, you seem comfortable with deadlines, but sometimes you do drop the ball.

- I'd like to see you be more consistent in terms of meeting or exceeding your deadlines.

- What can I do to help you meet your deadlines? I want to see you succeed.

- If you are having difficulty meeting deadlines, let me know; I am always willing to help.

- As far as deadlines go, it's always better to underpromise and overdeliver.

- We've given you all the tools you need to meet your deadlines. Are you not using them?

- I've never seen you meet a deadline yet. Does this bother you at all?

- It's very simple: you don't meet deadlines because you are giving yourself permission to do so.

- You seem to think that we set deadlines here just for the fun of it.

- You treat deadlines as though they were optional, but they most certainly are not.

- The fact that you can't ever make deadline is starting to cost us time and money.

- Deadlines are to you what kryptonite is to Superman.

- Trust me—no one here will hold it against you if you get your work done on time. [*sarcasm*]

- Don't you just love the sound of deadlines as they go whooshing by? [*sarcasm*]

Critical

Appraise an Employee's Time Management

Praising

- You approach every aspect of your work with punctuality, alacrity, and excellent time management.

- I love how methodical and organized you are. You really make each second count!

- I've never once seen you fail to make good use of your time here.

- All the talent and experience in the world is useless if you don't manage your time well.

- In general, I think you use your time well and wisely, but there is still room for improvement.

- We've all had issues managing our time. How can we best help you get the hang of this?

- I'd like to monitor the way you use your time more closely to get a more accurate picture.

- A big part of time management is planning your day. Let's try that and see what happens.

- There are so many programs and apps to help with time management. Let's look at some.

- Either you handle your time or it's going to handle you. It won't happen by magic, though.

- You seem a bit confused about the concept of good time management. Let me help fill in some blanks.

- If you don't learn how to manage your time better, we'll need to look into other alternatives.

- I need you to work smart, not just hard.

Critical

- If you had a handle on your time management, you wouldn't be so stressed.

- Procrastinating *or* burning yourself out with overwork will cost you dearly in your career.

- We do not pay you to fritter away your time here. Either step it up or you're through.

- If I had a dollar for every hour that you've wasted here, I'd be rich.

- Without a doubt you've taken time mismanagement to a whole new, *low* level.

- Perhaps you would be more comfortable in a job that doesn't require any time management skills—if there is such a thing.

Appraise an Employee's Attention to Detail

Praising

- You have a talent for sifting through even the most extraneous details of every situation.

- Your eye for details is impressive. You don't miss a thing, do you?

- You always seem to understand the truism that God is in the details.

- The fact that you are so detail-oriented makes you very good at what you do.

- I know that I can always count on you to see the finer points of every situation.

- Not everyone is able to focus on the details the way you do. Keep up the good work!

- You do a decent job of picking up on the details, but I think you could be a bit more thorough.

Critical

- It seems like you miss important details fairly often. What can we do to change this?

- No one expects you to catch every single detail, but you really need to make some improvements.

- Paying attention to the smallest details is an important aspect of your job. Can you do this?

- I don't care if you can't see the forest if all the trees are accounted for.

- I don't pay you for the big picture. I pay you to deal with all the minutiae so I don't have to.

- Just because they are "details" doesn't mean they are insignificant. I'm not sure what's unclear about that.

- I'm not sure you have the kind of mind-set that will enable you to work with this level of detail.

- If you can't take things down to the granular level, I'm not entirely sure why I hired you.

When an Employee Is Lazy

Lax

- I know it's tough to keep up one's energy. Maybe you should have some coffee or something.

- I don't care how unmotivated or lazy you are, as long as the work gets done in the end.

- I know it's difficult to get motivated sometimes, but I'd like to see you try harder.

- What can I do to help get you motivated, energized, and back on track?

- You get your work done, but I wish you were less lackadaisical in the execution.

- You seem to do the least amount of work possible just to squeak through.

- Your laziness is causing others on the team to have to take up your slack.

- No one expects you to be a superhero; just do the best you can and stop slacking off.

- I shouldn't have to constantly be prodding you to get your work done.

- Your laziness is just your way of saying that someone else will step in and get the job done.

- When I look at you, unfortunately I see a lazy and apathetic worker.

- The fact that you do no work undermines everything the *real* workhorses are doing.

- If you don't light a fire under yourself soon, I will have to do it for you.

- I'm not sure why you always seem to need to rest and take breaks when you're not even tired.

- So, I am supposed to pay you for basically acting as a chair-warmer all day long? [*sarcasm*]

- I didn't think it was possible for someone to have a more abysmal work ethic.

- Since when did sleeping on the job become a part of your job description?

- You are by far the least motivated employee I have ever had the misfortune of hiring.

- I so rarely have the opportunity to meet a man of leisure. [*sarcasm*]

Punitive

When an Employee Procrastinates

Tolerant

- We all procrastinate. Look—I'm doing it right now by talking to you! [*joking*]

- I have no issue with you procrastinating, as long as everything gets accomplished in the end.

- I don't care if you're a slow starter, as long as you finish everything you need to.

- Sometimes people procrastinate because they work well under pressure. Is that true for you?

- Nothing is so demoralizing as the eternal hanging-on of uncompleted tasks.

- Sometimes it seems difficult for you to begin projects. How can I help you dive right in?

- Why put off until tomorrow what you can do today?

- Procrastination is really just a bad habit. Here are some ways to break that habit once and for all.

- I am growing concerned that you put off onerous tasks until they become unmanageable.

- Procrastination is the art of keeping up with yesterday, and you're not even doing that.

- The others are getting tired of waiting for you to get off your butt and actually do some work.

- Were you considering putting off this meeting, too? [*sarcasm*]

Punitive

When an Employee Is Burned-Out

Concerned

- I know burnout when I see it. Please take some time off to regroup and refresh.

- I can see that you are really at the end of your rope. What can I do to help?

- I can see that you're running on empty. Maybe you should take a few days off to recharge.

- I feel badly that you are so burned-out. Have I been dumping too much work on you?

- You seem a little burned-out. What can I do to help you get back to top form?

- If you are feeling burned-out, you need to let someone know so that we can adjust your workload.

- The best antidote for burnout is to schedule your time wisely and take short breaks throughout the day.

- Most people get burned-out when they are not managing their time well. Is that the case here?

- We all get burned-out from time to time. It's just a fact of life in this fast-paced world.

- If you are overloaded with work, it's probably because you cannot say no to anyone.

- Everyone crashes now and then, but it's the way that it's handled that counts.

- I'm sorry you're feeling tapped out, but as they say, the show must go on.

- I think burnout is just a fancy way of saying you're too lazy to actually finish your work.

Critical

- I don't hire quitters, and I don't expect you to quit on me now, either.

- There is a reason we have a pot of coffee going all day. I suggest you make use of it.

- I guess you really don't have what it takes to succeed in this pressure cooker. What a pity.

- You need to stop and smell the Red Bull.

When an Employee Is Having Personal Problems

Compassionate

- I place the very highest importance on my employees' happiness. What can I do to help?

- What we do here is secondary to the real stuff of life. Please take as much time as you need.

- I've been through this, too, so I'd like to do what I can to help you through this difficult time.

- I know you're suffering greatly. Is there anything I can do to help?

- You don't need to tell me anything. Just know that I'm here if you need to talk.

- We have a program available through HR for people who are experiencing personal problems.

- If you are that overwhelmed with your personal issues, perhaps you should take a sabbatical.

- We all have personal problems, but it's important that we not allow them to affect our work.

- Take some time to get yourself together, but then please get back to the job at hand.

Critical

- There are times when you must put your emotions aside, especially if you want to succeed here.

- Your personal issues have been difficult for both of us, no doubt.

- You think you have problems? You should hear what's been going on in *my* life! [*joking*]

- Life is 10 percent what happens to you and 90 percent how you react to it.

- I feel badly saying this, but we can't afford to keep picking up the slack for you much longer.

- The other employees are starting to get frustrated that I'm cutting you all this slack.

- Sometimes I think you are using these life challenges as a crutch or an excuse. I hope I'm wrong.

- I need to know that I can still count on you, regardless of what's going on at home.

When an Employee Has Health Issues

Compassionate

- Your health is more important than anything. Please take care and get better soon.

- When it comes to health issues, they take top priority. Please take all the time you need.

- I'm sure you'll be back as soon as you are able. Please take as much time as you need.

- Your health is more important than anything, even the bottom line.

- Please take good care of yourself and get well soon. The work can wait.

Distancing

- I feel terrible that you're going through this. Please let me know if there's anything I can do.

- I've gone through a similar situation, so I know how you feel.

- Whenever you feel like coming back to work, please let me know. You'll be missed.

- Boy, it's a good thing we switched to a better insurance provider, isn't it?

- I feel terrible you're going through this, but I do have a department to run.

- Of course you know we'll need documentation from your health provider.

- I know you're ill, but would you at least consider working from home?

- Of course we'll do what we can, but meanwhile I'll need to find someone else to fill in.

- Unfortunately, these health issues are hampering productivity. Do you have any suggestions?

- So, what's the problem this time?

When an Employee Complains About the Workload

Empathic

- Nearly everyone feels overwhelmed from time to time. How can I help?

- Let's figure out a way to redistribute the work and help you get a handle on things.

- I am sorry you are feeling swamped. Let's look into making things a bit more manageable.

- I certainly understand that you're struggling. How can I help you manage more effectively?

- A complaint is an opportunity to make things better. How can I make things better for you?

- Nobody said it would be easy, but I promise you that the rewards will be well worth the effort.

- I know it's tough, but just hang in there. There is light at the end of the tunnel, I promise.

- This, too, shall pass.

- When the going gets tough, the tough need to get going.

- We all have a great deal to handle here. Perhaps it's a motivational or time-management issue?

- Everyone has a lot of plates up in the air, but complaining about it is counterproductive.

- Instead of complaining about it, why don't you look into brainstorming some positive solutions?

- If you focused as much energy on working as you do on complaining, you'd be in good shape.

- Life—and work—is 10 percent what happens to you, and 90 percent how you respond to it.

- We are all under quite a bit of pressure right now. Just keep your nose to the grindstone.

- Workers work; complainers complain. Now I guess I know which one you are.

- Complainers rarely get what they want, but they often get what they deserve.

- I could understand your negative attitude if you were handicapped in some way.

- If you can't cut the mustard, perhaps you should look into another line of work.

Distancing

When an Employee Complains About Pay

Empathic

- Your complaints are entirely valid. Let me see what I can do to remedy the situation.

- It's important to me that my staff is well compensated. I will do my best to get you a raise.

- I know you deserve more than you're getting right now. Let me see what I can do to remedy that.

- I understand why you would feel that way. Let's look into bumping up your salary a bit.

- Right now I think you're earning about what you're worth. Do you think you deserve more?

- I want to do this for you, but first I need to see how you perform over the next quarter.

- Sure, you're a talented team player, but your stock goes down each time you complain.

- If you really deserve to be in a higher tax bracket, then you'll need to prove it to me!

- Don't worry, your time for a raise will come soon. Just hang in there a bit longer.

- I know that you have it in you to deserve a raise and more, if you just worked a bit harder and smarter.

- If you want us to show you how much we value you, you first need to provide added value to us.

- Before you run your mouth about compensation, you should first ascertain if you deserve what you're getting now.

- If you worked as hard as you complain, you'd be the top earner around here.

Rejecting

- I'd like to be able to give you more, but it's just not in the cards right now.

- Your work should not be contingent on whether you're making as much as the person next to you.

- If you feel your pay is subpar, perhaps you should take it up with HR.

- In order for me to reward you for your good work, first you'll need to actually *do* some good work.

360 Degree Feedback

This multisource method of review and feedback is a popular (and sometimes unpopular) technique that some companies use for both development and appraisal purposes. For our purposes, we will use the term to denote the "upward review," when subordinates review their bosses. Remember when you finally had the chance to score the performances of your professors in high school or college? This is a similar concept. Ideally, this kind of feedback should always be given anonymously, so that subordinates can feel free to speak the truth without fear of reprisal.

If you decide to incorporate this practice into your management toolbox, just make sure you're not opening yourself to the opinions and recommendations of your direct reports unless you're actually prepared to listen to them. Otherwise, you risk creating a lot of dashed hopes and potentially resentful employees–hardly the result you were hoping for.

Appraise a Manager's General Management Skills

Praising

- He is by the far the most dedicated, empathic, and skilled manager I've ever had.

- Without her management acumen, I think we would all founder as a department.

- I don't usually say this, but he has been an inspiration to me.

- It is unusual to find a manager with such a fortuitous combination of smarts, drive, and empathy.

- Thanks to his guidance, I have been able to take my work to an entirely new level.

- Our success, both as individuals and as a department, is testament to her ability to lead.

- As managers go he's pretty good. At least, he doesn't get in our way.

- I think she tries her best, but sometimes the department feels like a rudderless ship.

- He's always busy, so he probably does a lot for the company. I'm just not sure what that is yet.

- We probably could have done most of the work without her, and done it better to boot.

- This type of "management" creates more impediments than it circumvents.

- I think he means well, but I just don't think he is management material.

- I think we would better off with someone with a fresh vision and approach.

- We certainly get a lot done when she isn't around.

Critical

- Sometimes I feel as though most of the problems in the department are created by him.
- She doesn't seem to really care about us as people.
- He is undoubtedly the source of all the problems in this department, and even this company.

Appraise a Manager's Coaching Skills

Praising

- There is simply no one else in the world who could have coached us to such great heights.
- She is the coach and mentor I always wanted in a boss but never had—until now.
- Because of his coaching, we have all grown as individuals and as a department.
- He has done more than give me a kick in the pants; he has given me a future.
- When she is around she provides good guidance, but sometimes I wish she were more accessible.
- I think he means well, but he doesn't seem to know how to bring out the best in his employees.
- Unfortunately, most of her "coaching" consists of pointing out everything we do wrong.
- I think he wants to think of himself as a mentor, but he doesn't know the first thing about coaching.
- As far as her coaching skills go, it's more "do as I say, not as I do."

Critical

- His coaching hasn't hampered things here, but it certainly hasn't helped us, either.

- It's tough to be a good coach when you don't even care about your employees.

- Coaching? *What* coaching?

Appraise a Manager's Project-Management Skills

Praising

- He is the reason we've been able to keep everything running through the pipeline smoothly.

- She is the one we count on to make sure that everything happens exactly as it should.

- Without him, I think we would be like a rudderless ship—destined to founder with each journey.

- Thanks to her skills and experience, we now have a smoothly running production process.

- There is simply no one else in the world who could manage our projects as well as she does.

- Without his direct involvement, this whole operation would implode.

- She is the main reason we are able to keep on track and on schedule consistently.

- Project management can be learned, but I'm unsure if he is willing to invest the time or energy.

- We could get everything done just as well, if not better, than when she is around, "managing."

- It's still really unclear who is supposed to be doing what around here.

Critical

- With his management style, chaos and disorder reign. How will we ever dig out of this mess?
- We need someone to come in here and tell us how to get things done.

Appraise a Manager's Interpersonal Skills

Praising

- Her greatness as a manager is evidenced in how she relates to her team as human beings.
- The way he relates to us as people is one of the reasons we would walk through fire for him.
- The great thing about her is that she not only leads, but she listens.
- He is a skillful manager, but he also takes the time to get to know us as people.
- I feel supported and encouraged by her at every turn.
- He has an amazing gift of leading while remaining a people person—a rare trait.
- She never neglects the human aspect of what she does.
- He is fairly good with people, so I don't really have any complaints in that regard.
- I believe she means well, but sometimes she's a bit lacking in the interpersonal skills area.
- What he lacks in the people skills department, he makes up for in productivity.
- Sometimes it seems as though a chip is missing from the "people skills" area of her brain.

Critical

- He definitely commands respect, but he isn't really liked as a person around here.

- Unfortunately, I can't give her high marks for her people skills, as they could use a lot of work.

- A huge part of managing is understanding the human quotient, but he just doesn't get that.

- I don't see any evidence that she even thinks of her direct reports as people, with emotions, problems, and challenges of their own.

- When he shows up in the morning, it's "duck and cover."

Appraise a Manager's Delegation Skills

Praising

- As capable as he is, he understands that he can't carry the world all by himself.

- We trust her because she trusts us enough to delegate even the most important tasks.

- He is like Tom Sawyer: he makes us *want* to take on even the most onerous tasks.

- She has the uncanny ability to assign work without anyone feeling burdened or resentful.

- Thanks to his skillful delegation, this department has become much more productive.

- She is a superstar leader because she allows each one of us to shine.

- His trust in us is evidenced in his willingness to off-load important tasks.

- She seems to hoard the more interesting projects, but that doesn't happen very often.

Critical

- Sometimes I think that he would prefer to just handle everything on his own.

- If she would just let us handle critical tasks, I think she would find things working more smoothly.

- I wish he would allow each of us to pull more of our own weight around here.

- She obviously thinks we are all incompetent, which is why she never delegates tasks to us.

- He basically hoards all the cool projects and then blames us when we don't feel motivated.

- She is stressed all the time because she prefers to micromanage and handle everything herself.

- I want to help, but he simply refuses to unload any tasks to others. It's like he doesn't trust us.

- We all stand around here, waiting for work, while she runs around like a chicken without its head.

Appraise a Manager's Hiring Skills

Praising

- She has a real talent for hiring exactly the right person for the job, each and every time.

- He is really a master at picking out the best people.

- She hires slowly and fires quickly, which is exactly what one needs to do as a manager.

- He instinctively knows that this company is only as good as the people it keeps.

- Like Lee Iacocca, she hires people who are smarter than she is and just gets out of their way.

- He has a knack for ferreting out the best talent and most advantageous fit, each and every time.

- She has a real eye for talent, and it shows in the fabulous team she's assembled here.

- He always seems to hire very solid, competent people.

- Sometimes she rushes through the hiring process, and, as a result, there have been a few bad apples.

- He is suspicious of candidates who are smarter, better educated, or more skilled than he is.

- She's a good manager, but she seems to flounder a bit when it comes to finding competent candidates.

- A manager is only as good as his team. I'm not sure what that says about him, unfortunately.

- We've been having some bad bad luck with new hires lately. Hopefully, it's just a phase.

- She lets her personal biases and issues get in the way of finding quality people.

- I'm not sure he's equipped to be taking part in the hiring process, let alone making the final decision.

- I wouldn't trust her to hire someone to clean our toilets; that's how bad things are.

Critical

Appraise a Manager's Leadership Skills

Praising

- Rather than dividing and ruling, as most managers do, he unites and leads us.

- She is the rare manager who understands that "to lead is to serve, nothing more, nothing less."

- He is a leader of integrity, energy, compassion, and foresight. We are lucky to have him.

- If a leader is a dealer in hope, that is why I feel hopeful when I get up for work every day.

- Because of his unimpeachable leadership, we would all be willing to walk through fire for him.

- I've never seen anyone so adept at garnering support and rallying the troops.

- I know I can always trust her to go ahead and forge a path for us when the going gets tough.

- He has managed to unite a really diverse team and lead us on to great things.

- She brings out the best in each and every one of us, which is what makes her a great leader.

- He's a good leader, but sometimes I wish he were a bit more involved.

- She sometimes abdicates her responsibility as a leader. I know she is capable of so much more.

- He seems more interested in the perks of leadership than the responsibilities that go with it.

- She would rather be our friend than actually run the department.

Critical

- His "leadership" has only managed to muddy the waters and confuse everyone in the process.

- Leadership? What leadership?

- There is no reason to rank her leadership skills, as I have yet to see her demonstrate any.

Appraise a Manager's Planning Skills

Praising

- He is that rare combination of a visionary *and* a planner.

- Her vision for the department shows in the concrete, well-thought-out plans she outlines for us.

- He always has each week—no, each *day*—planned down to the very minute.

- We are able to focus on the details because she has already planned out the big picture.

- So much of our work depends on good planning, which is why we've been so successful under him.

- She is a natural planner at heart, which is why we always have something interesting to do.

- His extensive planning is what has enabled us to meet and surmount every challenge.

- Sometimes she doesn't think far enough ahead, which leaves us vulnerable to surprises.

- It seems like things here just happen "organically," without any real planning or direction from above.

Critical

- He doesn't seem to understand that when you fail to plan, you may as well plan to fail.

- It seems like she just hopes that everything will eventually get done—but nothing ever does.

- Planning of any kind is definitely not his forte.

When a Manager Is Being Unethical

Understanding

- Well, most of life is lived in the gray area, not in black and white, right?

- Ethics is really a slippery slope that we all find ourselves sliding down from time to time.

- I really shouldn't throw the first ethical stone unless I am without sin, which I am not.

- Times are tough all around, so it's understandable that he'd be tempted to cut corners.

- I am sure this was just a one-off behavioral anomaly that won't be repeated.

- Sometimes she plays a bit fast and loose with ethics, but other than that, I have no complaints.

- I wish I could say that his values align with the common good, but unfortunately, I can't.

- Management should be held to a *higher* standard when it come to ethics.

- If he just straightened up and flew right, he would actually be a decent manager.

- Ethics cannot be taught; you either get it or you don't. Unfortunately, she doesn't.

- I'm not sure how she gets away with such shady behavior on the job.

More Harsh

- I fear for this company's future, given his lack of ethics and moral judgment.

- She is perhaps the most unethical manager I have ever had the displeasure of working for.

- I can no longer continue to work here, as I can't in good conscience condone his unethical behavior.

- All the good she does for this company is eclipsed by the underhanded way she accomplishes it.

- He is so ethically and morally bankrupt, I wonder if he is a sociopath.

When a Manager Plays Favorites

Understanding

- I don't mind that she plays favorites because I am one of them.

- It's understandable that he would favor the more talented of the bunch.

- We all try our best to get into her good graces, but only a few have been accorded that privilege.

- He seems to encourage his employees to curry his favor, which personally I find revolting.

- She has her special little clique, but the rest of us are just poor minions to be ignored.

- So-and-so can do no wrong with him. The rest of us are just lightning rods for his wrath.

- She means well, but the way she favors certain employees creates resentment and jealousy.

Critical

- It's sometimes difficult to ascertain who is in his good graces and who is on the outs.

- The lack of fairness and equality with which she treats the staff has created a lot of problems.

- He seems to enjoy playing favorites and pitting team members against one another.

- We all naturally gravitate toward certain people, but she needs to bring more fairness to the table.

- I hate how she takes only certain, special people under her wing, and the rest of us are basically ignored.

- Why should a certain select few get all the access to him, while the rest of us are persona non grata?

When a Manager Is Too Friendly With the Team

Appreciative

- His friendly management style has created a relaxed, happy place to work.

- Her friendliness wouldn't work with every team, but we all seem okay with it.

- He is definitely a fun person, but sometimes I wish we were more businesslike around here.

- I think she takes the friendliness a bit too far sometimes. Other than that, she is a great manager.

- I think it's important to have a bit more professional distance between yourself and your team.

- Her overfriendliness is not winning her any points in my book.

- It's tiresome to have to banter with the boss when all you want to do is get your work done.

- The overfriendly atmosphere in the department is neither healthy nor productive.

- Things here just seem too ingrown, incestuous, and dysfunctional.

- We do much better work when he's not around; he distracts us by trying to be everyone's friend.

- By trying to be everyone's friend, she's only succeeded in alienating all of us.

- Being polite and amicable is one thing, but the intense closeness she exhibits with her employees just feels wrong.

- If he were a little more hand-off, I think he would have a lot more of our respect.

- I think she is too close to us emotionally to be able to judge our performance objectively.

- He is just too nice, and the staff is starting to take advantage of that.

Critical

When a Manager Is Too Laissez-Faire

Appreciative

- It's okay to not be a disciplinarian as long as there is respect left at the end of the day.

- He has definitely "spared the rod," but it hasn't seemed to spoil the team too badly just yet.

- I have nothing against a "management light" approach, but hers may be a bit *too* light.

- I appreciate the fact that he trusts us to do the work, but I would prefer more involvement on his part.

- We would respect her more if she were a bit more hands-on with us in terms of results.

- Honestly, when he actually gives his opinion on something, we are all surprised.

- He couldn't be less involved if he didn't even work here.

- I understand the rationale for her lax approach, but she's not getting the best out of us that way.

- In terms of his management style, I'd like to see more MBWA: managing by walking around.

- She doesn't seem to understand that her absence implies a lack of caring and investment.

- Sometimes I get the feeling that he just doesn't care what goes on here.

- By failing to lead, he is essentially abdicating his right and responsibility as a manager.

- Here, it's basically a case of the lunatics running the asylum.

- We don't know what strong leadership is because we've certainly never seen it coming from her.

Critical

When a Manager Micromanages

Understanding

- Her management style, while a bit hands-on for some, has been effective for the most part.

- Some people call his management style tyrannical, but I just call it involved and invested.

- Yes, the micromanaging can be a bit oppressive at times, but at least we know she cares.

- I love that he is so engaged with the process, but sometimes it feels a bit stifling.

- If she just backed off and trusted us a bit, I know she could be a really great manager.

- By managing every little detail, he's taken away our incentive to succeed on our own.

- By focusing on the excruciating minutiae, all she does is waste time and ruffle feathers.

- If we get anything done, it's in spite of, not because of, his overbearing management style.

- Sometimes I get the feeling that she just doesn't trust us to handle anything important.

- We get more done when he's not around, throwing a monkey wrench into every situation.

- We're all scared to make a move because no matter what we do, we get punished.

- She is choking the life out of the team by making us account for every little thing.

- A little more air and room to breathe would suit us better, I think.

- I know we could do great things if we had a sense that he trusted us to get the job done.

Critical

- What she calls managing, we just call interfering and micromanaging.

- The lack of initiative and morale on this team is directly attributable to his micromanagement.

- No one enjoys being under the microscope 24/7, but that is how all of us feel right now.

When a Manager Is a Bully

Understanding

- I would probably resort to bullying tactics, too, if I had to manage this team!

- There are a lot of loose cannons around here, so I guess he feels he needs to rule with an iron fist.

- I can understand why she would feel the need to inspire a little fear in us from time to time.

- I get what he's trying to do, but he's really just shooting himself in the foot by bullying us.

- I think she does this out of fear and a lack of self-confidence, which is sad.

- His bullying belies all the lip service he gives about "respect" and a "supportive environment."

- None of us appreciates being essentially abused by our manager.

- She means well, but sometimes her directive behavior crosses the line into bullying territory.

- No manager is perfect, but I wish he were a bit kinder and less angry all the time.

- Productivity and morale are at an all-time low because of her bullying tactics.

Critical

- He thinks he is motivating us, but he is only shutting down the lines of communication.

- Her need to control everything and everyone has become a real problem for the company.

- Many managers resort to abusive tactics every now and then, but this is just ridiculous.

- This kind of behavior borders on the criminal. He should consider himself warned.

- When will she understand that being mean does not get the best out of your employees?

- He was probably bullied by his boss, which is why this is the only way he knows how to manage.

- Being tough is one thing, but being rough with one's inferiors is just demeaning to all concerned.

Index

About the Author

Patrick Alain is an internationally known video game developer. His titles include the number-one best-sellers "Grand Theft Auto," "Red Dead Redemption," and the *Midnight Club* series. He was born in Paris, France, and has lived in a number of countries throughout his life. Fluent in five languages, Alain attributes much of his success to his ability to function as a vital participant in large, multilingual teams. This book is the product of more than 10 years of experience in management. It is Alain's goal to share his knowledge regarding one of the most invaluable skills in life: *taking command in every situation.*

Alain lives in San Diego, California, with his wife and daughter. He holds a master's degree from the University of Paris.

PatrickAlain.com   Twitter.com/LeaderPhrases